Treasured Recipes
from the Charleston
Cake Lady™

Treasured Recipes from the Charleston Cake Lady™

Fast, Fabulous, Easy-to Make Cakes for Every Occassion

Teresa Pregnall

with Wally Pregnall and
Sara Sheppard Landis

Hearst Books   New York

It is the policy of William Morrow and Company, Inc., and its imprints and affiliates, recognizing the importance of preserving what has been written, to print the books we publish on acid-free paper, and we exert our best efforts to that end.

Library of Congress Cataloging-in-Publication Data
Pregnall, Teresa.
  Treasured recipes from the Charleston Cake Lady™: fast, fabulous, easy-to-make cakes for every occasion / Teresa Pregnall.
      p. cm.
    Includes index.
    ISBN 0-688-13931-0
    1. Cake.   2. Charleston Cake Lady™ (Charleston, S.C.)   I. Title.
TX771.P694   1996
641.8'653—dc20   95-47441
                                                                                                         CIP

Printed in the United States of America

First Edition

1 2 3 4 5 6 7 8 9 10

BOOK DESIGN BY LINDA KOCUR

This work is dedicated
with my best love
to the memory of my husband,
William Osgood Pregnall

My warmest thanks to:

Allison Engel and Margaret Engel, co-authors of FOOD FINDS, for giving us our first push and for their ongoing support.

Marian Burros, food editor for THE NEW YORK TIMES, for giving us our second push.

My charming and delightful editor, Jennifer Williams, whose help, cooperation, and enthusiasm have inspired my self-confidence and made the writing of this book so pleasant. In the world of editors I'm sure I have had the best.

Sadie Green, our wonderful Sadie, who has always been ready to help.

Teresa Gavitt, Ellen Whetsell, and Annette Kelly, my nieces, for pulling us through several major crises.

The many food editors for the magazines and newspapers across the country who have mentioned our cakes.

The political science professors at the College of Charleston who were always willing to eat the reject cakes. Their enthusiastic support was warmly welcomed.

And, last but not least, thanks to Wally, the brainchild of the Charleston Cake Lady. He has always been my number-one supporter.

Very special thanks to Sara Sheppard Landis whose warm support and literary talents have known no bounds. Without her encouraging words, her knowledge of the publishing world, and her spirit of helpfulness, the Charleston Cake Lady book might never have seen the light of day. Thanks, Sara, from my heart.

contents

❧

introduction

When I was asked to write this book, my first response was, "I don't have time. I'm too busy." But I thought again. I began to reflect on the pleasure I had derived from a lifetime of baking and preparing desserts, not to mention the fun and excitement that has come to me as the Charleston Cake Lady. So I decided to share some of that pleasure.

I got my start as the Charleston Cake Lady through good luck, and an army of friends. It all began in 1984 after my husband, Billy, retired. We wanted a small home-based business, and since I had always enjoyed baking, I suggested that we try taking cake orders. I concluded that the slogan "Do what you love" applied to me. I reasoned that, at the very least, if the business were a failure, I would still have fun doing it. But Billy had little interest in baking, so the idea didn't especially appeal to him, and for a while he argued against it. Finally he agreed. My aim was to start off small and try to sell a few of my cakes locally by taking orders for them. But it wasn't exactly that simple. I soon learned that in order to be licensed by the state of South Carolina I would have to have a separate kitchen. Of course, we didn't have one, and I feared that my bright idea was suddenly no longer quite so bright. But my dear husband jumped right in, as was his style, and built the kitchen for me. Little did we know that our small project was about to take off.

About a year later, we stumbled onto a newly published book, FOOD FINDS by Allison Engel and Margaret Engel, that listed and described all kinds of unique foods available through mail order. I wrote to the publisher and received an immediate response from Allison, asking me to send her a cake. I sent a poppyseed cake, and that was the beginning of our friendship. She was encouraging, supportive, and almost as enthusiastic about my cakes as I was. In fact, she contacted me several months later to ask if she could include our cakes in an article she was writing for THE WASHINGTON POST on mail-order gifts for Christmas. We decided to give the uncharted world of mail order a chance.

From Allison's one article we received about three hundred orders, and from those we gained many repeat customers and spin-off orders. The next year, Marian Burros, a veteran food editor at THE NEW YORK TIMES, heard about our cakes and mentioned them in her Christmas roundup. She was also kind enough to mention us in one of her books, 20-MINUTE MENUS. Things really snowballed without our even having to advertise our cakes. The next year, an article in USA TODAY was followed by articles in COUNTRY LIVING, THE WASHINGTONIAN, and

VICTORIA magazine. Since then, Allison Engel and her sister, Margaret Engel, have published a second edition of FOOD FINDS that includes us. Needless to say, this publicity has given us all the business we can handle. After filling each season's holiday orders, I swear "Never again," but my energy and enthusiasm are always restored by my customers.

The Charleston Cake Lady has continued to operate on a small scale for a variety of reasons, the most important of which is maintaining personal contact with my customers. I consider many of my regular customers good friends, or extended family, and I look forward to hearing from many of them several times a year so we can catch up with the events in our lives. Being able to maintain the personal touch is the most rewarding "business" aspect of my lifelong hobby.

And it really has been lifelong! My "baking career" began when I was a little girl. Like many Lowcountry families, we spent our summers at our beach home, where there were always more guests than residents. Those really were the "good old days," when most of our time was spent either having fun or planning the next fun thing. I was at my happiest when the house overflowed with people.

It was during these summer fun times that I first tried my hand as a baker. Some of the recipes I learned and enjoyed then are still family favorites, and they are included in this book.

All was not rosy at first. I shall never forget the first chocolate layer cake I tried to assemble. The occasion was a neighborhood beach party, which, we thought, would not be complete without an old-fashioned chocolate layer cake. Well, the layers came out "just right," and the icing was "just right," but the assembly was a disaster. By the time I had covered the first layer with a mound of chocolate icing and put the second layer in place, the cake began to crack. Novice that I was, I simply filled the crack with more icing. After much crack filling, it seemed time to place the third layer on top. Layer number three cracked worse than layer number two. I used more icing, then more, and even more! The end result was a huge cake with almost as much icing as cake. It was a smash hit with all the chocolate lovers, but the baker was exhausted. It was a hard way to learn not to bake such thick layers.

My baking experiences did not end with summer fun. As I tried recipes and experimented on my own, I gradually became the "dessert person" in our household. My family definitely carried on the Southern tradition of having dessert at every meal, so nobody ever complained when my concoctions appeared.

When I married into the Pregnall family, I couldn't believe the delicious "sweets" that were customary—breakfast buns, tea scones, cakes, pies, pudding, homemade ice cream. My mother-in-law, Katie Sheppard Pregnall, had two specialties to which I quickly became addicted. One was a lemon sponge cupcake that literally melted in your mouth. The cake was feather light and the lemon filling was smooth and tart. Her other specialty was the traditional Charleston wafer. She was well known for her wafers in Charleston, but I had never seen or tasted one until I met Billy. To watch her make those little treasures delicately spiced with cinnamon and nutmeg was an education in itself. Using a pair of long-handled antique irons six inches in diameter and joined at the top with a hinge, she made the most wonderful crunchy rolled wafers. After heating the irons to an intense heat on top of her stove, she would pour the light, rich wafer batter onto the bottom iron and cook the first side. Then she reversed the irons to cook the other side. While the wafer was still hot and flexible, she removed it from the irons and rolled it quickly with a knife. Haste was of the essence here since the rolled wafer crisped very quickly. The process was time-consuming and must have been backbreaking but what a delicious memory she left us. Her sister, Aunt Sadie (Sadie Sheppard Martin), made a mouthwatering Lady Baltimore cake—white layers with a richly delicious vanilla filling chock-full of chopped figs, raisins, nuts, and cherries and topped with a fluffy white icing.

Unfortunately, none of us ever learned how to make these specialties but we are still enjoying the memories.

Although my husband had been exposed to the very best from his mother and Aunt Sadie, he was nonetheless very complimentary to his young bride and always acted as though he enjoyed my desserts. So I continued to serve them at every meal. Small wonder we did not all gain weight.

During the first energy crunch in 1972, I began multiple baking. In an effort to conserve energy, I would bake two cakes at a time, one for us to eat and one to give away. And I learned to keep extras in my freezer. During this time I was working in the Alumni Affairs Office at the College of Charleston and would often carry the extra cake to the office. There were a number of student workers who helped us, and they were always hungry. Many of those former students are some of my best friends today. The only complaint I ever heard was from the director of Alumni Affairs, who claimed the crumbs attracted ants.

It was not until I transferred to the Political Science Department at the college that my cake baking became a serious matter. The professors and the staff always seemed to enjoy eating my cakes—even the rejects—and they were always generous in their praise. (Ants were not an issue.) Life there was happy. This kind of hospitality is part of the heritage for which the Old South is known.

Charleston cuisine is based on family recipes that were brought to the colonies by Englishwomen when Charles Town was first settled in 1670, and that were later enriched by Huguenot, German, and African dishes. Of course, our baking reflects many generations of handwritten and carefully saved "receipts" handed down from mothers to daughters through the years.

As one of those daughters, I have taken pride in learning to follow these recipes well. Since the art of cooking and baking is a way of life for me, I have changed and simplified many of the recipes and I am now happy to share them with you.

notes on ingredients,equipment, storage, and shipping

❧

although there is a short introduction to each section of this book, I'd like to share a few little "words of wisdom" I have learned over the years.

ingredients

Always use the freshest ingredients available. On a rare occasion that sour cream or yogurt shows up in our bakery after its expiration date it goes in the trash. My advice is to buy what you need when you need it. Many of the house brands are good and sometimes they are a few cents cheaper than brand names. Just be sure that the product is fresh.

Be very careful in making substitutions. It is perfectly all right to use skim milk wherever milk is listed; but if you substitute fresh milk for evaporated milk or vice versa the taste will be slightly different, so that is not a good change to make.

References to flour are usually plain flour. In those rare instances when a recipe calls for self-rising flour it will be clearly stated. References to sugar always mean granulated sugar. Brown sugar and confectioners' sugar are always clearly indicated.

With respect to butter, margarine, sour cream, and yogurt, please be careful. Substitutions in these can be tricky and are not usually recommended. The low-fat and nonfat versions of these products are wonderful "inventions" for calorie or fat-conscious dietary needs. But they don't perform too well in the oven. They tend to cause coarseness and drying out and they often hinder the cake's rising capabilities. It is better to use the real thing, have a successful dessert, and serve smaller portions.

equipment

You will need several sizes of pans but unless you're already a baking enthusiast you won't need a lot of each size at first. For the many recipes for pound cakes or pound cake varieties, a 12-cup tube pan or Bundt pan is needed. The layer cakes are baked in 8-inch or 9-inch layer pans and you will need three of these. Most brownies, chews, and bars are baked in a 12 x 9-inch or 13 x 9-inch pan. Buy one of these. A cake rack and a cake tester are both essentials. And even though an electric mixer is not an absolute must, it is highly recommended since beating and creaming ingredients are vital to the success of many recipes.

I have electric ovens in one kitchen and gas ovens in the other kitchen. Both of them are acceptable, so I personally have no preference. The important thing is to have enough airflow in your oven. In other words, don't crowd the oven. A big pound cake needs lots of air around it.

storage

Unless it is otherwise indicated, most of our cakes can be stored at room temperature. (Of course, it stands to reason that a cake would be happier in the refrigerator than in a non-air-conditioned room on a ninety-degree day.) The cakes like to be covered with plastic wrap or kept in a cake cover. Brownies, cookies, chews, and muffins should be stored in an airtight container, and though it's not necessary, it is not unwise to wrap them in plastic wrap before putting in an airtight container.

The Charleston Cake Lady has several cake freezers. I do believe in freezing cakes—all of my cakes freeze beautifully. I'm really not a happy camper when the cake freezer is almost empty.

Just a few basic guidelines: No cake wants freezer burn, so be sure that it is properly wrapped. I usually use several layers of plastic wrap, making sure that no air is trapped inside. Place the wrapped cake in a heavy plastic food bag and secure it with a tie or with tape. Label and date the bag, then put it in the freezer. Cakes may be frozen whole or sliced, but since the slices tend to dry out more quickly, I feel that the whole cake survives freezer life better than sliced cake. I like to take even more precautions with brownies, muffins, and chews since they tend to become dry more easily. Wrap them in several layers of plastic wrap and put them in an airtight container before freezing.

shipping

Should you want to ship some of your newly baked goodies, here are a few of our tips.

Use a 200-pound corrugated box (these can be purchased at a packaging store).

Use enough Styrofoam popcorn or other suitable packaging fill (also available at packaging stores) to make sure that the item doesn't move in the box during rough handling.

Be sure that the address INCLUDING THE CORRECT ZIP CODE and your return address are clearly written on your mailing label. (Incorrect zip codes can cause serious delays.) Cover the mailing label with clear sealing tape so that it cannot become detached or smudged if it gets wet. It is also a good idea to stamp or write the word "perishable" on the box.

A number of dependable shipping services are available, most of them just a telephone call away. Federal Express is extremely dependable and gives good service. However, no ground service is offered by FedEx, so costs here are not cheap.

UPS offers ground service, as well as next-day air and second-day air. Since ground service is considerably less expensive than air service, it is wise to check rates and travel times before you ship. I highly recommend both of these companies.

Whenever possible, I ship perishables on Monday or Tuesday, seldom ever at the end of the week. This assures me that the package is delivered before the weekend. During holiday seasons shipment time slows down and it is necessary then to figure on at least one extra day in transit.

Preparing perishable items for shipping is a relatively easy procedure. And when you consider the recipient's delight it becomes even easier.

24

Best-sellers
from the
Charleston
Cake Lady™

about pound cakes

✣

as you move into the little world of the Charleston Cake Lady, you will note that pound cakes are held in high esteem and that the names of three very special people appear rather often in the recipe headnotes. Somehow I can't write about these wonderful baked treats without mentioning the folks who have helped me enjoy them. So, just a word about Billy, Wally, and Sadie.

Billy was my husband. He took care of us in a thousand different ways and, in his own special way, was my very best friend. Our lives revolved around him. In spite of his death in November 1993, he is still very much a part of our lives, our thoughts, our conversations, and, of course, our hearts. Wally is our son. A gentle, soft-spoken young man, he is the brainchild of the Charleston Cake Lady —and the apple of his mother's eye. As a colleague once said to me, "He's very definitely your Alpha and your Omega." Sadie is our housekeeper, cook, friend, confidante, and "boss." She has excelled in all of these categories for a half century, and although her health is frail now, her spirit is not. She runs a tight ship here and not one of us is foolish enough to question her authority. Our self-appointed hostess, she now much prefers answering the telephone to baking cakes or washing pans. We love her and can't imagine life without her.

As for the esteemed pound cakes, to say that they are very popular with us is an understatement. I've heard many people claim to have no success with pound cakes. I submit that they are indeed easy to make and these are my tips for success:

✦ Be sure to use butter (sweet) and/or margarine that is at room temperature. In almost all cases, margarine may be substituted for butter or vice versa, if you so desire, unless indicated otherwise.

✦ If you're using margarine, be sure to use the real thing. Do not use one of the light or reduced-fat varieties. Because they contain more water and/or oil than regular margarine they will cause the cake to be dry and coarse.

✦ ALWAYS cream the butter (or margarine) and sugar well—very well. This is extremely important.

✦ Be sure to beat the mixture well after the addition of each egg. Since it is so important to mix and blend the ingredients well, I strongly recommend using an electric mixer.

✦ I also recommend that pound cakes be placed in a cold oven.

- Testing for doneness is an absolute necessity. At the end of the prescribed baking time, insert a toothpick or cake tester into the middle of the cake; if it comes out clean, the cake is done. If the batter sticks to the tester, bake the cake for an additional five minutes, then test again. Test every cake you bake —not just pound cakes. It takes just a few seconds, and we all know the "better safe than sorry" story.

- Allow a pound cake to cool in the pan for about an hour before placing it on a cake rack. Then let it cool for several hours before it is served or stored. The length of cooling time is determined by the size of the cake; a large cake requires more cooling time than a smaller one does. If you are going to serve the cake right away, use a sharp cake knife or a kitchen knife with a serrated blade.

- If a cake is to be stored or frozen, it must be properly wrapped to prevent drying out and/or freezer burn. To store the cake, wrap it well in plastic wrap or foil and put it in a cool place. To freeze the cake, wrap it tightly in several layers of plastic wrap so that no air is left. Place the wrapped cake in a plastic food bag and close it securely. Protected in this way, the cake should stay fresh in your freezer for four to six weeks. All of the Charleston Cake Lady cakes freeze well. And isn't it nice to have something homemade on hand when unexpected visitors appear? By the way, sliced cake will thaw at room temperature in a matter of minutes.

- Feel free to substitute plain yogurt for sour cream in these recipes if you prefer, but DON'T USE THE NONFAT PRODUCTS since they tend to cause dryness.
- You can change the flavor of your cake by substituting or combining different extracts. For example, most people prefer the flavor of lemon extract in our Charlestowne Pound Cake, but I like it better when it is flavored with a mixture of vanilla and almond extracts.
- One last word. Most pound cakes, especially the ones included here, need no frosting. They are rich and wonderful by themselves, and they make great accompaniments for fruit, ice cream, frozen yogurt—the list is endless. I could go on forever extolling the virtues of the pound cake, but I shall now stop and let you begin. Good luck!

Special Pound Cake

My father thought there was nothing better than a slice of good pound cake. He was raised on a farm in upstate South Carolina, where there was seemingly an endless abundance of fresh foods. His family was large and, from all accounts, his mother must have baked a pound cake every day. When he left the farm and came to Charleston to attend medical school, he brought with him the idea that his mother made the world's best pound cake. Oddly enough, he never seemed to dwell on any of her other culinary feats, but the memory of her pound cakes was a powerful one.

Trying to replicate a cake my mother and I had never tasted was not easy, but we continued to try until we finally found the "right" combination of ingredients. I rather think that by then Daddy had forgotten what the original cake tasted like or had become confused by our many attempts. At any rate, he was pleased, and that was all that mattered.

2 cups all-purpose flour

2 teaspoons baking powder

1 cup sweet butter (do not substitute margarine), softened

1⅔ cups granulated sugar

5 large eggs

⅓ cup milk

1 teaspoon pure almond extract

Makes 18 thick slices

Do not preheat the oven. Grease and flour a 10-cup tube pan.

Sift together the flour and baking powder and set aside.

In a large mixing bowl, cream the butter and sugar until light and fluffy, about 5 minutes. Beat in 1 egg. Alternately add the flour mixture and milk, beating well after each addition. Beat in the remaining 4 eggs and the almond extract.

Pour the batter into the prepared pan and place it in a cold oven. Set the oven temperature to 325° and bake the cake for 1 hour, or until a cake tester inserted in the center of the cake comes out clean. Allow the cake to cool in the pan for about an hour before placing it on a cake rack. Cool for 3 hours before serving.

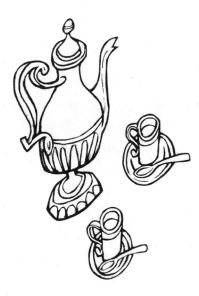

Charlestowne Pound Cake

Some time after we had duplicated our grandmother's cake for Daddy, his brother, Uncle Ferry, announced that he, too, wanted to find a pound cake that was like his mother's. He simply didn't believe that Daddy remembered what the legendary cake actually tasted like! So we started in with the pound cake trials all over again. When my Charlestowne Pound Cake was created I sent one to my uncle and he immediately made another announcement. The lost cake had been found—or so he thought. Amused, I wondered if my grandmother had had access to lemon yogurt in the 1800s. But Uncle Ferry dearly loved the Charlestowne Pound Cake and raved about it until he died at the age of ninety-four.

This cake was also the first entirely "original" to emerge from the Charleston Cake Lady commercial kitchen. And it didn't really have an official name until one of my customers fondly referred to it as the Charlestowne Pound Cake. That name stuck and it has been an extremely popular cake with friends, family, and customers. I was pleased that my uncle was happy with his found cake, especially since he was born on Daddy's seventh birthday, August 7, and they celebrated their birthdays together. This was a family holiday for as many years as I could remember, and no other cake could be served for their big day—THE birthday!

Be sure to follow the instructions carefully because this requires more beating than most cakes. Enjoy!

Do not preheat the oven. Grease and flour a 12-cup tube pan.

Sift together the dry ingredients and set aside.

In a large mixing bowl, beat the butter and sugar on low speed for 13 minutes until very creamy, scraping the sides of the bowl often with a spatula. Add the eggs one at a time, mixing for 1 minute after each addition. Add the dry ingredients in 3 additions alternately with the yogurt, scraping the bowl often and beating well after each addition. Add the lemon extract.

Pour the batter into the prepared pan. Place in a cold oven and set the oven temperature to 325°. Bake for 1 hour and 5 minutes, or until a cake tester inserted in the center of the cake comes out clean. Allow the cake to cool in the pan for about an hour. Place the cake on a cake rack and cool for 4 hours before serving.

3 cups all-purpose flour

1/2 teaspoon baking soda

1/4 teaspoon salt

1 cup sweet butter or margarine, softened

2 1/2 cups granulated sugar

6 large eggs

1 cup lemon yogurt

1/2 teaspoon pure lemon extract

Makes 20 large slices

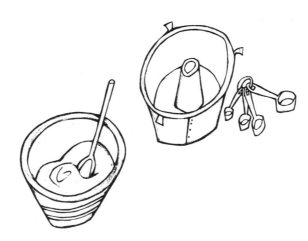

Confectioners' Sugar
Pound Cake

the use of confectioners' sugar in this cake causes the texture to be a little smoother than that of pound cakes containing granulated sugar. It is a dense cake and the combination of lemon and almond extracts provides an unusual flavor.

Do not preheat the oven. Grease and flour a 12-cup tube pan.

In a large mixing bowl, beat the butter and sugar on low speed until light and fluffy, about 10 minutes. Alternately add the eggs and sifted flour, beating well after each addition. Add the vanilla, almond, and lemon extracts and mix well.

Pour the batter into the prepared pan. Place in a cold oven and set the oven temperature to 325°. Bake for 1 hour and 5 minutes, or until a cake tester inserted in the center of the cake comes out clean. Cool the cake in the pan for about an hour, then remove the cake to a rack and allow the cake to cool thoroughly before slicing.

1 pound sweet butter, softened

1 box (1 pound) confectioners' sugar, sifted

6 large eggs

3 cups all-purpose flour, sifted

1 teaspoon pure vanilla extract

½ teaspoon pure almond extract

½ teaspoon pure lemon extract

Makes 20 large slices

Country Pound Cake

When we were children, my parents often took us to the country to visit Daddy's cousins. They lived on a huge farm in Bowman, South Carolina, and we looked forward to each visit. Daddy's aunt, Molly Weathers, was one of the best bakers in upper South Carolina, and the marvelous aromas of her fresh-baked bread, biscuits, cookies, and cakes still come wafting across time. This is one of her famous pound cake recipes.

Do not preheat the oven. Grease a 12-cup tube pan and line the bottom with wax paper.

Sift the dry ingredients together and set aside.

In a large mixing bowl, beat the butter, shortening, and sugar on low speed for 10 minutes. Add the eggs one at a time, blending well after each addition. Alternately add the dry ingredients and milk, mixing well. Add the vanilla and lemon extracts.

Pour the batter into the prepared pan. Set the oven temperature to 350° and bake for 1 hour and 20 minutes, or until a cake tester inserted in the middle of the cake comes out clean. Allow the cake to cool in the pan for 1 hour. Remove to a cake rack and cool for at least 3 hours.

3 cups all-purpose flour

¾ teaspoon baking powder

¼ teaspoon salt

1 cup sweet butter (do not substitute margarine), softened

½ cup solid vegetable shortening

2⅔ cups granulated sugar

5 large eggs

1 cup milk

1 teaspoon pure vanilla extract

1 teaspoon pure lemon extract

Makes 25 slices

Chocolate Pound Cake

the dense texture and deep chocolate flavor of this cake make it the ultimate dessert for chocolate lovers. Because it is so rich, the cake needs no frosting, but it is especially delicious served with vanilla ice cream.

Do not preheat the oven. Grease and flour a 12-cup tube pan.

Sift together the flour, baking powder, cocoa, and salt. Set aside.

In a large mixing bowl, beat the margarine and sugar on low speed until fluffy, about 8 to 9 minutes. Beat in the eggs one at a time, mixing well after each addition. Mix in the dry ingredients alternately with the milk. After each addition, scrape the bowl with a spatula so that all the ingredients are well distributed. Beat in the vanilla extract.

Pour the batter into the prepared pan. Place the pan in a cold oven and set the oven temperature to 325°. Bake for 1 hour and 20 minutes, or until a cake tester inserted in the middle of the cake comes out clean. Allow the cake to cool in the pan for at least 1 hour before removing to a cake rack to cool for at least 3 hours longer.

3 cups all-purpose flour

1/2 teaspoon baking powder

1/2 cup Dutch-processed cocoa

1/4 teaspoon salt

1 1/2 cups sweet butter or margarine, softened

3 cups granulated sugar

5 large eggs

1 1/4 cups milk

1 teaspoon pure vanilla extract

Makes 22 large slices

Crunchy Pound Cake

the confectioners' sugar in this cake gives it a smoother texture than conventional pound cakes made with granulated sugar. This delightfully smooth cake teams up with a crunchy topping to deliver an incredibly delicious taste. And it looks pretty too. Serve it with fresh fruit (I like a combination of sliced peaches and blueberries) or just slice and serve with coffee.

Do not preheat the oven. Grease a 12-cup tube pan.

In a small bowl, blend all the topping ingredients with a fork and press into the bottom of the prepared pan. Set aside.

In a large mixing bowl, blend the butter and sugar on low speed and beat until light and fluffy (approximately 5 to 6 minutes). Add the eggs one at a time, beating well after each addition. Slowly stir in the sifted flour. Add the vanilla extract.

Pour the batter into the prepared pan and bake for 1 hour at 325°, or until a cake tester inserted in the center of the cake comes out clean. Cool the cake in the pan for at least 1 hour. Invert the pan over a cake plate and view your beautiful crunchy pound cake. Enjoy.

topping

½ cup crushed vanilla wafers (14 wafers)

2 tablespoons melted margarine or sweet butter

½ cup pecans, finely ground

2 tablespoons granulated sugar

cake

2 cups sweet butter (use no substitute)

2 cups confectioners' sugar

7 large eggs

3 cups all-purpose flour, sifted

2 teaspoons pure vanilla extract

Makes 20 glorious slices

Cream Cheese Pound Cake

If you can imagine a pound cake that tastes like cheesecake, you will have a good idea of just how rich this pound cake really is. With its velvety-smooth texture and delicate cream cheese flavor, this cake is perfect by itself. However, if you would like extra-rich goodness, try the Cream Cheese Frosting on page 73.

Do not preheat the oven. Grease and flour a 12-cup tube pan.

Sift together the flour and salt and set aside.

In a large mixing bowl, cream the margarine, cream cheese, and sugar on low speed for 10 minutes, or until light and fluffy. Beat in the eggs alternately with the dry ingredients, mixing well after each addition. Add the vanilla.

Pour the batter into the prepared pan. Set the oven temperature to 325° and bake for 1½ hours or until a toothpick or cake tester inserted in the center of the cake comes out clean. Cool the cake in the pan.

3 cups all-purpose flour, sifted

¼ teaspoon salt

1½ cups margarine or sweet butter, softened

1 package (8 ounces) cream cheese

3 cups granulated sugar

6 large eggs

1½ teaspoons pure vanilla extract

Makes 20 generous slices

Pineapple Pound Cake

The tangy-sweet flavor of pineapple gives this pound cake an unusual twist. It's a delicious complement to a hot cup of tea, but it also makes a smashing dessert topped with vanilla ice cream or a dollop of whipped cream and a sprinkle of pecans.

Do not preheat the oven. Grease and flour a 12-cup tube pan.

Sift together the flour, baking powder, and salt. Set aside.

In a large mixing bowl, beat the butter and sugar on low speed until light and fluffy, about 10 minutes. Beat in the eggs one at a time, mixing for 1 minute after each addition. Alternately add the sifted dry ingredients and the milk, beating just until smooth. Add the vanilla extract. Fold in the drained pineapple.

Pour the batter into the prepared pan and set the oven temperature to 350°. Bake for 1 hour, or until a cake tester inserted in the middle of the cake comes out clean. Cool the cake in the pan.

Invert the cake onto a serving plate. For a finished look, dust the cake with sifted confectioners' sugar.

3½ cups all-purpose flour

2 teaspoons baking powder

½ teaspoon salt

1 cup sweet butter or margarine, softened

2 cups granulated sugar

6 large eggs

1 cup evaporated milk

2 teaspoons pure vanilla extract

1 cup canned crushed pineapple, drained

Confectioners' sugar for dusting (optional)

Makes 22 large slices

Mahogany Pound Cake

This is the perfect cake for brown sugar lovers. Mahogany Pound Cake is dense, moist, and super-good. The brown sugar and chocolate blend so beautifully that neither flavor is dominant. Try this unusually delectable cake with a scoop of vanilla ice cream.

Do not preheat the oven. Grease and flour a 12-cup tube pan.

Sift together the flour and cocoa. Set aside.

In a small bowl, stir the baking soda into the sour cream. Set aside.

In a large mixing bowl, cream the butter and both sugars until light and fluffy, about 10 minutes. Beat in the egg yolks one at a time, mixing well after each addition. Add the vanilla extract. Alternately add the sifted dry ingredients and sour cream mixture, mixing well. In a separate bowl, beat the egg whites until they are dry. Fold in the beaten egg whites until well blended.

Pour the batter into the prepared pan and set the oven temperature to 325°. Bake for 1½ hours, or until a cake tester inserted in the center of the cake comes out clean. Cool the cake in the pan.

2½ cups all-purpose flour

½ cup Dutch-processed cocoa

¼ teaspoon baking soda

1 cup sour cream

1 cup sweet butter or margarine, softened

2 cups granulated sugar

1 cup firmly packed dark brown sugar

6 large eggs, separated

1 teaspoon pure vanilla extract

Makes 20 large slices

about specialty cakes

Our wonderful customers have made us feel that all our cakes are special. But some of them are considerably more popular than others, and these have become our specialty cakes.

I debated whether or not to include a few of these recipes because they call for prepared mixes. As a dedicated baker, I am aware that purists frown on mixes, and, personally, I prefer to use my own ingredients. With this in mind, I made an effort to re-create these recipes completely from scratch. However, after many, many attempts at combining different ingredients in different proportions—none of which could hold cake textures at their peak for serving, storing, or shipping—I came back to the mixes (you can use the mixes of your choice; I like Duncan Hines). Since the Poppyseed, Gem, and Milk Chocolate cakes are the Charleston Cake Lady's most popular items, and because I know that many of our customers would be disappointed not to see them here, I have included the recipes.

Macaroon Cake is a fun variation on a favorite dessert. Everybody loves macaroons, but sometimes the occasion calls for something a little more formal. This cake is reminiscent of the simpler cookie, and the almond flavor adds depth and interest.

Vanilla Wafer Cake is a spin-off from another old Charleston favorite—Vanilla Wafer Pudding, which combines wafers, fruit, and custard. This cake is easier to serve and eat than the pudding, and the wafers give it an unusual texture and crispness.

I like to think that our fruit and vegetable cakes deviate a bit from the norm. In each of these recipes, we've taken the usual elements and, with a little imagination and experimentation, have turned the commonplace into something quite distinctive.

One look at Blackberry Wine Cake will make you want to plan your next dinner party just so you can show off this glamorous dessert. And just think of all the wonderful compliments you'll receive from your guests when you serve them the Charleston Cake Lady's Coconut Carrot Cake.

Our Fruited Spice, Applesauce, Banana-Pineapple, and Spice cakes all contain unusual and sometimes exotic combinations of fruit. Yet, once again, they are extremely easy to make and great fun to serve.

Nut cakes have long been favorites with Charleston hostesses because they are perfect for any occasion—from a simple tea to a family dinner to a lavish holiday party. There is probably no better and quicker way to add distinctive flavor, richness of texture, and crunch to your baked goods than to simply toss in a handful of nuts.

One of the Charleston Cake Lady's best-sellers, Sherry Nut Cake, combines the crunch of walnuts, the sweetness of nutmeg, and the subtle nutty flavor of sherry wine to transform a couple of simple mixes into a gourmet delight. Brown Sugar Nut Cake and Black Walnut Cake, both "made from scratch," are delightful and just as easy to make.

All of our specialty cakes are unique, yet, other than following simple directions, no special techniques are involved. Just mix the ingredients, set the oven to the right temperature, bake, test for doneness, and cool on a rack, then serve and enjoy! All of the specialty cakes keep beautifully and ship well.

Specialty cakes look so attractive when they come out of the oven that they don't need any adornment, and because they are so rich and moist, you don't need to frost them. Ice cream, frozen yogurt, fresh fruit, a simple sauce, or a delicate sprinkling of confectioners' sugar can turn these cakes into instant gourmet desserts for the most gala occasions.

Until now these specialties, which I've experimented with and tested for several decades, were available only from the Charleston Cake Lady, but now you can achieve the same results in minutes, and in your own kitchen, with my easy-to-make recipes.

Gem Cake

We always have a Gem Cake in the house. We love it, fancy or plain. The first time I tried to make this cake, though, it was a gigantic flop. The entire inside collapsed, leaving just a puffy outer ridge. When it was removed from the pan, the cake looked just like a soggy sun hat. I tried again and produced another hat—but this time we were able to taste enough of it to know that it was worth trying again. So I kept trying. And failing. After a great many failures, it became known as the Failure Cake. But I continued to try, and finally, after a few more attempts, a proper-looking cake emerged. No more sun hats!

Somewhat lighter in texture than pound cake, yet not as light as a chiffon cake, Gem Cake is absolutely scrumptious. Alone, it literally melts in your mouth. It can be paired with any number of fillings or toppings to make it into an even more fabulous dessert.

One of my favorite concoctions is Lemon Lush. Slice the cake diagonally to make three layers. Fill the layers with Dannon Lemon Chiffon Yogurt (use three 8-ounce containers). Cover the top and sides of the cake with whipped topping (12 ounces) and refrigerate. Another favorite: Make a double batch of Best Chocolate Icing (page 45). Fill the hole with frosting, then cover the top and sides of the cake generously with frosting (watch them fight over the hole!). Billy's favorite was a slice of Gem Cake covered with vanilla ice cream and topped with fresh fruit.

When we discovered how versatile, as well as delicious, it is, we renamed it Gem Cake. It is truly a gem.

Do not preheat the oven. Spray a 12-cup Bundt pan with cooking spray.

In a large mixing bowl, combine the cake mix, sugar, sifted flour, sour cream, and oil. Add the eggs and mix on low speed for 1 minute. Increase the mixer speed to medium-high and beat for 4 minutes, or until light and fluffy.

Pour the batter into the prepared pan. Set the oven temperature to 325° and bake for 50 minutes, or until a cake tester inserted in the middle of the cake comes out clean Cool the cake in the pan.

1 package (18.5 ounces) butter recipe golden cake mix

$1/3$ cup granulated sugar

1 tablespoon all-purpose flour

1 cup sour cream

$1/2$ cup vegetable or canola oil

4 large eggs

Makes 18 generous
slices

Macaroon Cake

this cake is for coconut lovers only! It is dense, moist, rich, and absolutely delicious. But it's temperamental and there are times when—no matter what—this cake just looks raggy. (Don't say I didn't warn you.)

No matter how it looks, Macaroon Cake is so rich and tastes so good, it needs no partner except a hot cup of tea or coffee. However, for a really spectacular dessert, serve it with lime sherbet.

Do not preheat the oven. Grease and flour a 10-cup tube pan.

In a large mixing bowl, beat the shortening and sugar on low speed for 5 minutes until creamy. Add the eggs one at a time, beating for 1 minute after each addition. Alternately beat in the sifted flour and coconut, mixing well. Beat in the almond extract.

Pour the batter into the prepared pan. Place it in a cold oven, set the oven temperature to 325°, and bake for 1 hour, or until a cake tester inserted in the middle of the cake comes out clean. Cool the cake in the pan.

1 cup Crisco (do not substitute)

2 cups granulated sugar

6 large eggs

2 cups all-purpose flour, sifted

8 ounces grated coconut (fresh or frozen)

1 tablespoon pure almond extract

Makes 18 big slices

Chocolate Chip Cake

describing my signature chocolate chip cake in her NEW YORK TIMES column, Marian Burros says, "Chocolate chips are everywhere in this three-pound cake." She's absolutely right. My cake adds a whole new dimension to the lowly chocolate chip. It is moist, not too dense, delicately flavored, and bursting with mini chocolate chips.

Preheat the oven to 325°.

Grease and flour a 12-cup Bundt pan.

In a large mixing bowl with a mixer, blend the cake mix, sugar, sour cream, and oil on low speed for 1 minute. Add the eggs one at a time, blending well after each addition. Increase the mixer speed to medium and beat for 4 minutes. Add the vanilla extract. Fold the chocolate chips into the batter by hand and stir gently until they are well distributed.

Pour the batter into the prepared pan and bake for 50 minutes, or until a tester inserted in the middle of the cake comes out clean.

Remove the cake from the oven and allow it to cool in the pan. Invert the cake onto a plate and enjoy your delicious chocolate chip cake.

1 package (18.5 ounces) butter recipe golden cake mix

$1/3$ cup granulated sugar

8 ounces sour cream (do not use low-fat or nonfat)

$2/3$ cup vegetable oil

3 large eggs

1 teaspoon pure vanilla extract

1 package (12 ounces) mini semisweet chocolate chips

Makes 18 generous slices

Poppyseed Cake

Charleston, our gracious Old World city, is at its loveliest at Christmas when the seventeenth-century homes are lavishly bedecked with holiday fruits, holly, and ivy. Every year throngs of Charlestonians and visitors alike line the streets of the Battery to view the annual Christmas Parade of Boats, a brightly lit flotilla that sails down the waterfront. And all along Rainbow Row, Meeting Street, and Tradd Street, hostesses prepare to welcome guests to early dinner, or perhaps to a light snack of homemade seed cake and a warming glass of sherry.

Seed cakes have been a mainstay of entertaining in Charleston ever since benne seeds came from Africa with the first slaves. These early African Americans believed the benne seeds brought them good luck, and although poppyseeds differ from benne seeds, many hostesses would agree today that the poppyseed has brought them good luck, especially when it is served in our poppyseed cake.

Not only a favorite in Charleston, our Poppyseed Cake is ordered again and again by people all over the country. I am told that one of our Poppyseed Cakes rivaled the star-spangled sky for attention at a recent Fourth of July party on Manhattan's East River.

Preheat the oven to 350°. Grease a 12-cup tube pan.

Combine all the ingredients in a large mixing bowl and blend on low speed for 1 minute. Increase the speed to medium and beat for 2 minutes.

Pour the batter into the prepared pan and bake for 45 to 50 minutes, or until the cake is golden brown on top and the sides have started to come away from the pan. Cool the cake in the pan.

This cake needs no frosting. It is good served for dessert or at any time of day.

Note: Poppyseed cake stores well and freezes well if properly wrapped. (See storage notes on page xix.) And because it ships well, Poppyseed Cake makes a special holiday gift. One Charleston Cake Lady customer, who used to live here but moved away, writes, "It's like a taste of home. I smell it and I'm back in Charleston at a gala party."

1 package (18.5 ounces) white cake mix

1 package (3³/₄ ounces) instant vanilla pudding mix

¹/₂ cup poppyseeds

1 cup vanilla yogurt

¹/₂ cup vegetable oil

¹/₂ cup sherry wine

4 large eggs

Makes 18 slices

Milk Chocolate Cake

Surprise and delight swept through the Charleston Cake Lady bakery when a beautiful color photograph of our Milk Chocolate Cake appeared in the Christmas 1992 issue of VICTORIA magazine. We simply weren't prepared for the avalanche of orders that poured in. It is still our number one cake, surpassing even our Poppyseed Cake in popularity.

Milk Chocolate Cake was created at the request of a dear friend who wanted a chocolate cake that was somewhat lighter than our Chocolate Pound Cake. After many unsuccessful attempts at making the cake from scratch, I began experimenting with a prepared mix. After considerable adjustments, I found the right combination. When it met with the taster's approval, his remark was "It tastes just like a candy bar!" Hence its name.

Deliciously light, yet deeply chocolaty, this cake has only one flaw: Nobody can eat just one slice. It needs no frosting, but for a special treat, try serving it with chocolate chip frozen yogurt.

1 package (18.5 ounces) butter recipe golden cake mix

3 tablespoons Dutch-processed cocoa, sifted

$1/3$ cup granulated sugar

1 cup sour cream

$2/3$ cup vegetable oil

3 large or 4 medium eggs

Makes 18 large slices

Do not preheat the oven. Spray a 12-cup Bundt pan with vegetable cooking spray.

In a large mixing bowl, combine the cake mix, cocoa, sugar, sour cream, and oil and beat on low speed just to blend. Add the eggs and blend well. Increase the speed to medium-high and beat for 5 minutes.

Pour the batter into the prepared pan and set the oven temperature to 325°. Bake for 55 minutes, or until a cake tester inserted in the middle of the cake comes out clean. Cool the cake in the pan.

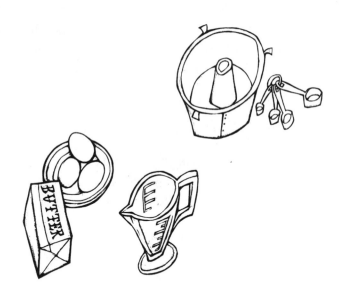

Vanilla Wafer Cake

I was introduced to this cake a few years ago, at a luncheon held at the College of Charleston and have been enjoying it since then. In this recipe, vanilla wafer crumbs blend with coconut and pecans to create an outrageously satisfying crunch that just can't be found in cakes made with flour. I like to serve it with ice cream—any flavor—but it really isn't necessary. The cake is truly heavenly by itself.

Preheat the oven to 325°. Grease and flour a 12-cup tube pan.

In a large mixing bowl, beat the margarine and sugar on low speed for 3 to 4 minutes until light and fluffy. Add the eggs one at a time, beating well after each addition. Add the crushed vanilla wafers alternately with the milk. Fold in the coconut and chopped pecans.

Pour the batter into the prepared pan and bake for 1 hour and 15 minutes, or until a cake tester inserted in the middle of the cake comes out clean. Cool the cake in the pan.

1 cup margarine or sweet butter, softened

2 cups granulated sugar

6 large eggs

1 box (12 ounces) vanilla wafers, crushed

½ cup milk

7 ounces grated coconut (fresh or frozen)

1 cup chopped pecans

Makes 18 generous slices

Sherry Nut Cake

ranking high in popularity with our Charleston Cake Lady customers is Sherry Nut Cake. At first I thought, how could I possibly like a recipe that contains a couple of prepared mixes? But I tried it and the rest, as they say, is history. The cake is light, nutty and spicy. It goes very well on a party tray or a breakfast buffet, and it is excellent with coffee or hot tea. I have often baked it in mini pans and served small slices as dessert tidbits on a fancy plate at parties and teas.

I have baked sherry nut cakes for about thirty years and have never had a failure. So, in addition to its fabulous taste and versatility, it can be declared failproof.

Preheat the oven to 350°. Grease a 12-cup tube pan.

In a large mixing bowl combine all the ingredients except the nuts and beat on low speed for 1 minute. Increase the speed to medium and beat for 5 minutes. Add the nuts and beat on low speed until the nuts are well distributed, about 1 minute.

Pour the batter into the prepared pan and bake for 50 minutes, or until the cake is brown on top and comes away from the sides of the pan. Cool the cake in the pan.

1 package (18.5 ounces) yellow or white cake mix

1 package (3¾ ounces) instant vanilla pudding mix

2 teaspoons grated nutmeg

¾ cup sherry wine

¾ cup vegetable oil

4 large eggs

1 cup chopped pecans or walnuts

Makes 18 generous slices

Brown Sugar Nut Cake

If you like brown sugar, you will love this cake. Our Brown Sugar Nut Cake is rich, dense and loaded with brown sugar. A few customers who don't care for nuts have requested the cake without them. They tell me it tastes delicious without the nuts. Either way, this is a fabulous cake. I like to serve it with vanilla frozen yogurt or ice cream.

This is a very large cake, but leftovers freeze extremely well—so don't let its size keep you from making it. Just wrap and freeze a portion of it for a later date.

$3^{1}/_{4}$ cups all-purpose flour

$^{1}/_{2}$ teaspoon baking powder

1 cup pecans, finely chopped

$1^{1}/_{2}$ cups margarine or sweet butter, softened

2 cups firmly packed dark brown sugar

1 cup granulated sugar

5 large eggs

1 cup milk

1 teaspoon pure vanilla extract

Makes 22 large slices

Do not preheat the oven. Grease and flour a 12-cup tube pan.

Sift 3 cups of the flour and the baking powder together. Set aside.

In a small bowl, toss the nuts with the remaining ¼ cup flour. Set aside.

In a large mixing bowl, combine the margarine and dark brown and granulated sugars and beat on low speed until creamy, about 5 minutes. Add the eggs one at a time, mixing well after each addition. Alternately add the sifted dry ingredients and milk. Mix well. Beat in the vanilla. Gently fold in the floured nuts.

Pour the batter into the prepared pan and set the oven temperature to 325°. Bake for 1 hour and 25 minutes, or until a cake tester inserted in the middle of the cake comes out clean. Cool the cake in the pan.

Black Walnut Cake

black walnuts are wonderfully rich and have their own special flavor. They are also hard to find, which makes this cake a rare treat. It is rich and dense, and the taste is beyond description.

The only time black walnuts are available in Charleston supermarkets is during the holiday season, so I try to buy and freeze as many as I can afford. I always chop or grind the walnuts before freezing them, so they are ready for instant use.

3 cups all-purpose flour

1 teaspoon baking powder

1 cup black walnuts, finely chopped

1 cup sweet butter (do not substitute margarine), softened

1/2 cup margarine, softened

3 cups granulated sugar

5 large eggs

1 teaspoon pure vanilla extract

1/2 teaspoon rum flavoring

1 cup whipping cream or half-and-half

Makes 20 large slices

Do not preheat the oven. Grease and flour a 12-cup tube pan.

Sift together 2½ cups of the flour and the baking powder. Set aside.

In a small bowl, toss the nuts with the remaining ½ cup flour. Set aside.

In a large mixing bowl, beat the butter, margarine, and sugar on low speed until light and fluffy, about 10 minutes. Beat in the eggs one at a time, mixing well after each addition. Add the vanilla and rum flavorings and mix well. Alternately add the sifted dry ingredients and cream, ending with the flour mixture. Using a rubber spatula, gently fold in the floured nuts.

Pour the batter into the prepared pan and set the oven temperature to 325°. Bake for 1 hour and 20 minutes, or until a cake tester inserted in the middle of the cake comes out clean. Allow the cake to cool in the pan.

Fruited Spice Cake

In case you don't remember being introduced to Sadie, our housekeeper/boss, I will have to say a word about her here, since she is somewhat responsible for this cake. Sadie has been cooking for us for fifty-two years, and she reigns supreme in our kitchen, a fact I learned to accept years ago when my son, Wally, was quite young. One of his little friends got his hand slapped for "peeping into one of Sadie's pots." The child was not particularly impressed, but the incident left a lasting impression on me. I not only don't peep, I listen when she speaks.

So, when Sadie insisted that I try her simple version of carrot cake (see page 78), my feelings were ambivalent. Never having thought that baby food was so wonderful, I did not find the idea of including it in a recipe particularly appealing. But one doesn't reject Sadie's suggestions, so I tried the cake and was in fact pleasantly surprised. Some time later, I decided to experiment, and the end result was our Fruited Spice Cake. The baby food gives it a fruity flavor and helps keep the cake extra-moist. It makes a good breakfast treat because it is not too sweet.

I have sold Fruited Spice Cake to hotels and inns, for their continental breakfasts, as well as to individual customers. One of these, a computer analyst, orders a Fruited Spice Cake for each of her new clients. She says it's a good way to say, "Thanks for your business." I think it's a good way to enjoy a tasty snack. Try a big slice with a cup of hot tea.

Preheat the oven to 350°. Grease and flour a 10-cup tube pan.

In a large mixing bowl, stir together the dry ingredients. Add the oil, eggs, and baby food and mix well. Gently fold in the nuts.

Pour the batter into the prepared pan and bake for 1 hour, or until the top is golden brown and the sides come away from the pan. Cool the cake in the pan.

2 cups self-rising flour, sifted

2 cups granulated sugar

1 teaspoon grated nutmeg

1 teaspoon ground cinnamon

1 cup vegetable oil

3 large eggs

1 jar (4 ounces) baby food plums

1 jar (4 ounces) baby food peaches

1 jar (4 ounces) baby food pears

1 cup chopped pecans or walnuts

Makes 18 generous slices

Coconut Carrot Cake

Customers tell us that our Coconut Carrot Cake is most unusual. It was developed for a special customer in Washington, D.C., who claimed to be a coconut expert, and who wanted a coconut cake with "a different twist." The amount of carrot is just enough to provide a little extra crunch and flavor—and the cinnamon adds a pleasant spiciness. Our client was delighted, and the cake met with such great popularity that we offered it for many years. This is the first time I've been willing to share my secret. I hope you enjoy it.

Preheat the oven to 350°. Grease and flour a 12-cup tube pan.

Sift together the flour, baking powder, cinnamon, and salt. Set aside.

In a large mixing bowl, combine the sugar, oil, and beaten eggs and mix well. Add the dry ingredients and mix just until blended. Add the vanilla extract. Fold in nuts, coconut, and carrots.

Pour the batter into the prepared pan. Bake for 1 hour, or until a cake tester inserted in the middle of the cake comes out clean. Cool the cake in the pan.

2 cups all-purpose flour

2 teaspoons baking powder

1 tablespoon ground cinnamon

½ teaspoon salt

2 cups firmly packed light brown sugar

1½ cups vegetable oil

4 large eggs, beaten

1 teaspoon pure vanilla extract

1 cup chopped pecans or walnuts

1 cup grated coconut (fresh or frozen)

½ cup grated carrots

Makes 18 generous slices

Blackberry Wine Cake

t his is our most "talked about" cake! Its luscious glaze and delicate orchid color make it beautiful to look at. And, of course, it gets raves for its fabulously rich taste. But it is super-sweet, so serve small slices.

Preheat the oven to 350°. Grease a 12-cup tube pan.

Sprinkle the nuts evenly over the bottom of the pan. Set aside.

In a large mixing bowl, blend the cake mix, gelatin, oil, wine, and eggs on low speed for 1 minute. Increase the speed to medium-high and beat for 5 minutes.

Pour the batter into the prepared pan. Bake for 45 to 50 minutes, or until the top of the cake is brown and the sides have come away from the pan.

While the cake is baking, prepare the glaze in a medium mixing bowl. Combine the melted and cooled margarine and the wine. Gradually stir in the confectioners' sugar until the mixture is smooth.

Remove the baked cake from the oven. With a fork, cover the entire surface of the cake with deep holes. Pour the glaze over the hot cake. Let it cool in the pan for about 1 hour.

Invert the glazed cake onto a pretty plate and serve.

1/2 cup pecans, finely chopped

1 package (18.5 ounces) white cake mix

1 package (3 ounces) blackberry gelatin

1/2 cup vegetable or canola oil

1/2 cup blackberry wine

4 large eggs

glaze

1/2 cup margarine or sweet butter, melted and cooled

1/2 cup blackberry wine

2 cups confectioners' sugar, sifted

Makes 18 delectable slices

Applesauce Cake

here's a cake that is easy to bake and even easier to eat. A customer in the gift basket business orders this cake made into mini loaves. She says they are some of her most popular basket stuffers, not only because of the cake's delicious taste, but also because of its long shelf life. I can attest to the taste but not its longevity, since none has ever lasted long around here. It is dense, quite moist, and deliciously spiced. I usually serve it with fresh hot coffee, and without frosting or other accompaniment.

Do not preheat the oven. Grease a 12-cup tube pan.

Sift together the flour, baking soda, baking powder, cinnamon, allspice, and salt. Set aside.

In a large mixing bowl, combine the applesauce, sugar, water, melted margarine, and egg. Mix on low speed for 1 minute, or stir with a wooden spoon, until well blended. Fold in the nuts and raisins until well distributed.

Pour the batter into the prepared pan and set the oven temperature to 350°. Bake for 1 hour and 5 minutes, or until a cake tester inserted in the middle of the cake comes out clean. Cool the cake in the pan.

$2^1/_2$ cups all-purpose flour

$1^1/_2$ teaspoons baking soda

$^1/_4$ teaspoon baking powder

1 tablespoon ground cinnamon

1 teaspoon ground allspice

$^1/_4$ teaspoon salt

1 jar (16 ounces) unsweetened applesauce

2 cups granulated sugar

$^1/_2$ cup water

$^1/_2$ cup margarine or sweet butter, melted

1 large egg

$1^1/_2$ cups chopped walnuts or pecans

$1^1/_2$ cups raisins

Makes 18 good-sized slices

Banana Pineapple Cake

We first offered Banana Pineapple Cake to our customers about ten years ago, and it met with instant success. Because it is so popular, we've kept it on the menu. Everyone who tastes this cake—even those of us who aren't crazy about bananas—agrees that it is absolutely delicious.

The bananas and pineapple in this recipe join forces to give the cake its incredible moistness, and the cinnamon adds a delicate spicy flavor. This cake enjoys a good shelf life and freezes well too—if there's any left to freeze, that is.

Preheat the oven to 350°. Grease and flour a 12-cup tube pan.

Sift the flour, baking soda, cinnamon, and salt into a large mixing bowl. Stir in the sugar.

Add the bananas, pineapple, oil, eggs, and vanilla and stir with a wooden spoon until well blended, about 60 strokes. Or use an electric mixer and blend on low speed for approximately 1 minute.

Pour the batter into the prepared pan and bake about 1 hour, or until a toothpick or a cake tester inserted in the middle of the cake comes out clean. Cool the cake in the pan.

3 cups all-purpose flour

1 teaspoon baking soda

1 teaspoon ground cinnamon

1/4 teaspoon salt

2 cups granulated sugar

2 cups chopped bananas (about 3 medium bananas)

1 cup canned crushed pineapple, well drained

1 1/4 cups vegetable oil

3 large eggs

1 teaspoon pure vanilla extract

Makes 18 irresistible slices

Spice Cake

With so many different spice cake recipes around, it is hard to pick a favorite. I've included this one, however, because it is a fabulously delicious cake and the ingredients are relatively healthful.

Because it is so very dense and moist, this cake needs no frosting. It makes a great breakfast treat or a tasty, nutritious snack at any time of day. Try it with a cup of freshly brewed hot tea.

Preheat the oven to 325°. Grease a 13 x 9-inch pan.

Sift together the flour, baking soda, baking powder, cinnamon, allspice, and salt into a large bowl.

Add the sugar, applesauce, yogurt, egg substitute, and oil and stir until well blended. Fold in the raisins.

Pour the batter into the prepared pan and bake for 45 minutes, or until a cake tester inserted in the middle of the cake comes out clean. Cool the cake in the pan, then cut it into $1^{1}/_{2}$-inch squares.

$2^{3}/_{4}$ cups all-purpose flour

$2^{1}/_{2}$ teaspoons baking soda

$1^{1}/_{4}$ teaspoons baking powder

1 teaspoon ground cinnamon

$^{1}/_{2}$ teaspoon ground allspice

$^{1}/_{2}$ teaspoon salt

$2^{1}/_{4}$ cups granulated sugar

$1^{3}/_{4}$ cups unsweetened applesauce

$1^{1}/_{4}$ cups plain nonfat yogurt

$^{1}/_{2}$ cup egg substitute

$^{1}/_{3}$ cup canola oil

1 cup raisins

Makes 48 squares

Charleston
Classics

about charleston classics

❦

the intent of this book is not to talk about "Olde Charlestowne" but to share the fun and excitement of the Charleston Cake Lady. The collection of recipes would not be complete, however, without a little something reminiscent of our gracious old city. So the next few pages will include a few of our Charleston classics. They speak to our love of good food and our enjoyment of family and friends. Some of these recipes have been handed down for many years. Some are new variations on old favorites. All of them are truly classics and are to be enjoyed everywhere, not just in Charleston.

Chocolate Chip Cheesecake

Wally once had a girlfriend who said she had never met a cheesecake she didn't like. Her reaction to this one was "That's the cheesecake to fight for!"

Extremely rich—ultra-delicious! Serve it to your extra-special guests.

Preheat the oven to 300°.

In a small bowl, combine the crushed cookies and melted butter, stirring to blend well. Press the cookie crumb mixture evenly over the bottom of an ungreased 9-inch springform pan. Set aside.

In a small bowl, mix the flour and ½ cup of the chocolate chips. Set aside.

In a medium bowl, beat the cream cheese until fluffy. Gradually add the milk and beat until smooth. Stir in the eggs and vanilla extract, mixing well. Stir in the flour mixture and blend well.

Pour the batter into the prepared pan. Sprinkle the remaining ½ cup chips evenly over the top.

Bake for 1 hour, or until the top is lightly brown. Cool the cake in the pan.

When the cake is thoroughly cooled, remove the side of the pan and slice the cake. Store leftovers in the refrigerator.

1½ cups finely crushed oreo cookies (18 to 20 cookies)

¼ cup sweet butter, melted

1 teaspoon all-purpose flour

1 cup mini semisweet chocolate chips

3 packages (8 ounces each) cream cheese, softened

1 can (14 ounces) sweetened condensed milk

3 large eggs, beaten

2 teaspoons pure vanilla extract

Makes 12 small slices

Best Devil's Food Cake

In an attempt to ward off an acute chocolate attack several years ago, I concocted this recipe and it soon became a family favorite. Sadie decided to try her hand at it as a birthday surprise for me, and when she read the note I'd written to myself, "Beat like crazy," she decided that crazy beating was the key to the cake's light texture. Perhaps she was right. In any case, the cake is extremely light and chocolaty and it is sinfully rich.

Preheat the oven to 325°. Grease and flour three 8-inch layer cake pans.

In a large mixing bowl, beat the cake mix, oil, water, and yogurt until blended. Add the eggs one at a time, mixing on low speed for 1 minute after each addition. Scrape the sides of the bowl well, then increase the speed to medium-high and beat for 5 minutes. Add the almond extract and blend on low speed for 1 minute.

Pour the batter into the prepared pans. Bake for 15 to 20 minutes, or until the cake comes away from the sides of the pans. Allow the layers to cool for 25 minutes, then invert the layers onto a cake rack to cool thoroughly before icing the cake.

1 package (18.5 ounces) devil's food cake mix

1/2 cup vegetable oil

1/2 cup water

1 cup vanilla yogurt

3 large eggs

1/2 teaspoon pure almond extract

Makes 16 slices

Best Chocolate Icing

Sift the sugar and cocoa together.

In a large mixing bowl, cream the butter on low speed for 1 minute. Alternately add the sugar-cocoa mixture and the milk, blending well. Add the vanilla extract, increase the mixing speed to high, and beat for 5 minutes, or until spreadable.

Frost the cooled cake with the icing.

To assemble the cake, place 1 thoroughly cooled layer upside down on a cake plate and spread with a thick layer of icing. Top with a second layer and spread with a thick layer of icing. Place the third layer on top and generously spread the top and sides of the cake.

4 cups (1 box) confectioners' sugar

3/4 cup unsweetened cocoa

1/2 cup sweet butter or margarine, softened

1/2 cup evaporated milk

1 teaspoon pure vanilla extract

Makes 6 cups

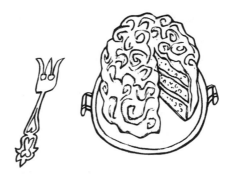

Lowcountry Nut Cake

a term often heard in our part of the world is "Lowcountry," which refers to the low-lying coastal stretch of land that extends from the Carolinas to Georgia. "Lowcountry" in a recipe title simply means it is a longtime regional specialty. Even though this particular recipe is full of nuts, its texture is light—the perfect partner for a glass of sherry or a cup of fresh fruit.

Do not preheat the oven. Grease and flour a 12-cup tube pan.

Sift together $2\frac{1}{2}$ cups of the flour, the baking powder, and salt. Set aside.

In a medium bowl, toss the nuts with the remaining $\frac{1}{2}$ cup flour. Set aside.

In a large mixing bowl, beat the butter and sugar on low speed until light and fluffy, about 5 minutes. Add the eggs one at a time, beating well after each addition. Alternately add the flour mixture and milk. Add the vanilla extract. Gently fold in the nuts until evenly distributed.

Pour the batter into the prepared pan and set the oven temperature to 350°. Bake for 45 minutes, or until a cake tester inserted in the center of the cake comes out clean. Cool the cake in the pan.

3 cups all-purpose flour

1 tablespoon baking powder

$\frac{1}{4}$ teaspoon salt

2 cups finely chopped mixed nuts (I use walnuts, pecans, and black walnuts)

1 cup sweet butter or margarine, softened

2 cups granulated sugar

4 large eggs

1 cup milk

1 teaspoon pure vanilla extract

Makes 20 large slices

Old South Nut Cake

the recipe for this old-fashioned nut cake was handed down to me from my grandmother. My family always served it during the Christmas holidays, but now I serve it year-round. It is especially good with a cup of coffee or a glass of cold milk.

Do not preheat the oven. Grease and flour a 12-cup tube pan.

In a small bowl, toss the nuts with ½ cup of the sifted flour. Set aside.

In a large mixing bowl, beat the butter and sugar on low speed until light and fluffy, about 10 minutes. Alternately add the eggs and the remaining 2½ cups sifted flour, blending well after each addition. Add the vanilla extract. Fold in the nuts with a spatula just until evenly distributed.

Pour the batter into the prepared pan. Set the oven temperature to 300° and bake for 1½ hours, or until a cake tester inserted in the middle of the cake comes out clean. Cool the cake in the pan for 1 hour.

Remove the cake to a cake rack and allow to cool thoroughly. Store the cake in an airtight container.

2¾ cups mixed nuts, finely chopped

3 cups self-rising flour, sifted

1 cup sweet butter (do not substitute margarine), softened

1½ cups granulated sugar

6 large eggs

1 tablespoon pure vanilla extract

Makes 22 slices

Heavenly Coconut Cake

This cake is wonderfully rich by itself, but if you serve it with Coconut Sauce, it becomes an exotic dessert. Just remember to serve small slices since it is so rich.

Preheat the oven to 325°. Grease and flour a 12-cup tube pan.

Mix the nuts and coconut in a small bowl. Sprinkle this mixture over the bottom and sides of the prepared pan.

In a large mixing bowl, combine the cake mix, pudding mix, oil, water, and cream of coconut and blend on low speed for 1 minute. Add the eggs one at a time, blending well after each addition. Increase the speed to medium and beat for 2 minutes.

Pour the batter into the prepared pan and bake for 1 hour, or until the cake comes away from the sides of the pan.

Prick the hot cake all over with a fork. Pour half of the Coconut Sauce over the cake. Allow the cake to cool in the pan.

Invert the cooled cake onto a plate and cover it with the remaining sauce. Let the cake cool thoroughly before slicing.

½ cup pecans, finely chopped

⅓ cup finely grated fresh coconut

1 package (18.5 ounces) yellow cake mix

1 package (3¾ ounces) instant vanilla pudding mix

½ cup vegetable or canola oil

½ cup water

½ cup cream of coconut

4 large eggs

Makes 20 slices

Coconut Sauce

In a small saucepan, combine the butter, sugar, and water, bring to a boil, and boil for 1 minute. Remove the pan from the heat and stir in the cream of coconut. Use immediately.

1/2 cup sweet (unsalted) butter

1/3 cup granulated sugar

2 tablespoons water

3 tablespoons cream of coconut

Makes 1 cup

Punch Bowl Cake

this could be considered a trifle but it has been called punch bowl cake ever since I can remember. Every time I make it, I am reminded of the advice I got from a wise old lady: "If you want to be popular, wear a red dress and stand beside the punch bowl!"

The very name of this cake puts me in a party mood, and when you serve it, you'll be popular even without the red dress. It's especially beautiful in a sparkling crystal bowl, and people will be back for seconds and even thirds. It's easy to make too.

Prepare the cake mix according to the package directions, making 2 round layers. Bake, then let cool.

Mix the pudding according to the package directions. Set aside.

Crumble one of the baked cake layers into a large glass bowl. Add half of the pudding, half of the pineapple, 1 banana, and all of the blueberry pie filling. Crumble the second cake layer on top and layer with the remaining pudding, pineapple, and banana. Top with the cherry pie filling. Cover with the whipped topping and sprinkle with the coconut. Chill for at least 1 hour before serving.

1 package (18.5 ounces) white cake mix

1 package (6 ounces) vanilla pudding mix (not instant)

1 can (20 ounces) canned crushed pineapple, drained

2 large bananas, sliced

1 can (21 ounces) blueberry pie filling

1 can (21 ounces) cherry pie filling

1 container (16 ounces) frozen whipped topping, thawed

1 cup grated fresh coconut

Makes 24 servings

Carolina Orange
Date-Nut Cake

during the holidays in Charleston, this cake is often served right beside traditional fruitcakes. I think it was originally developed as a Christmas cake for all those folks who don't care for the candied fruit in fruitcake.

Do not preheat the oven. Grease and flour a 12-cup tube pan.

Sift together the flour, baking soda, and baking powder.

In a medium bowl, toss the nuts and dates with ½ cup of the flour mixture.

In a large mixing bowl, beat the butter and sugar on low speed for 8 minutes, or until light and fluffy. Add the eggs one at a time, mixing well after each. Alternately add the remaining flour mixture and the buttermilk, mixing well. Stir in the orange extract. Fold in the nuts and dates.

Pour the batter into the prepared pan and set the oven temperature to 300°. Bake for 2 hours, or until a cake tester inserted in the center of the cake comes out clean.

While the cake is baking, prepare the sauce.

Combine all of the ingredients and bring to a boil. Remove from the heat and pour over the hot cake. Cool completely in the pan before serving.

4 cups all-purpose flour

1 teaspoon baking soda

1 teaspoon baking powder

1 cup pecans, chopped

1 package (8 ounces) chopped dates

1 cup sweet butter, softened

2 cups granulated sugar

4 large eggs

1½ cups buttermilk

1 teaspoon pure orange extract

Makes 22 large slices

sauce

1½ cups granulated sugar

1 cup fresh orange juice

1 teaspoon pure orange extract

Makes 3 cups

Cranberry Banana Pie

Cranberries aren't just for Thanksgiving and Christmas anymore. This year-round dessert delivers great holiday flavor—with just the right cranberry tang—any time. And it's pretty too!

In a small bowl or cup, soften the gelatin in the water for 5 minutes. Place the container in a pan of hot water and stir over low heat to dissolve the gelatin (or dissolve it in a microwave oven for 30 seconds). Set aside.

In a medium bowl, mix together the cranberry sauce, lemon juice, and lemon zest. Stir in the dissolved gelatin. Fold in the bananas. Pour the mixture into the baked pie shell.

In a small mixing bowl, beat the cream with the sugar on high until it holds firm peaks. Spread the whipped cream over the top of the pie. Garnish with additional banana slices, if desired (best to slice them just before serving). Store in the refrigerator.

Note: To reduce calories, replace the whipped cream with 2 cups frozen whipped topping, thawed.

1 envelops (0.25 ounce) unflavored gelatin

¼ cup cold water

1 can (16 ounces) jellied cranberry sauce

1 tablespoon fresh lemon juice

1 teaspoon grated lemon zest

2 ripe bananas, very thinly sliced, plus additional for garnish

One 9-inch frozen pie shell, baked and cooled

1 cup heavy cream, whipped

2 tablespoons granulated sugar

Makes 8 large slices

Gardenia Pie

t he recipe for this pie was given to me by a colleague at the College of Charleston. She told me that years ago it was known in her family as vinegar pie, but that her mother, being a true Southern belle, changed the name to gardenia pie, explaining that it always reminded her of afternoon tea parties in Charleston gardens.

Simple to make, this delicious dessert will make any meal a special one.

Preheat the oven to 325°.

In a medium bowl, combine the sugar, salt, eggs, vinegar, and melted butter and stir just until blended. Add the nuts, raisins, and coconut and mix well.

Pour the batter into the unbaked pie shell. Bake in the bottom third of the oven for 30 minutes, or until the top is lightly browned. Cool thoroughly before cutting. Store in the refrigerator.

1 cup granulated sugar

1/4 teaspoon salt

2 large or 3 medium eggs, beaten

2 tablespoons white vinegar

1 tablespoon sweet butter, melted

1/2 cup chopped pecans

1/2 cup raisins

1/2 cup grated coconut (fresh or frozen)

One 9-inch frozen pie shell

Makes 8 slices

Coconut Pie

because so many Charleston recipes contain coconut, we sometimes have to disguise a dessert for the non—coconut lovers among us. Not so for this pie. One doesn't even have to like coconut to enjoy it. It is dense, delicious, and oh-so-easy to make.

Preheat the oven to 350°.

In a medium bowl, beat the eggs with a fork or wire whisk until foamy. Stir in the sugar, milk, vanilla extract, and melted margarine until blended. Stir in the coconut.

Pour the batter into the unbaked pie shell. Bake for 45 minutes, or until the filling is set. Allow to cool before slicing. Store in the refrigerator.

3 large eggs

¾ cup granulated sugar

¾ cup milk

1 teaspoon pure vanilla extract

2 tablespoons margarine, melted

1 cup grated coconut (fresh or frozen)

One 9-inch frozen pie shell, thawed

Makes 8 large slices

Chocolate Chess Pies

We have some of the country's best neighbors here in the Lowcountry. I happen to think that I have THE best. Whenever my neighbor (she's eighty-four years old) bakes these pies, my family is usually the recipient of the second one. What a delightful, delicious way to say "Hi, neighbor!" Yet, it's one of those easy-to-do, never-fail concoctions. And it's sinfully delicious.

Preheat the oven to 350°.

Bake the pie shells for 5 minutes. Set aside. (Leave the oven on.)

In a medium bowl, combine the beaten eggs, sugar, sifted cocoa, evaporated milk, and melted butter and stir until well blended. Add the vanilla extract.

Spoon the mixture into the pastry shells. Bake for 45 minutes, or until the centers are firm to the touch.

Let cool. Makes two 9-inch pies.

Two 9-inch frozen pie shells

4 large eggs, beaten

3 cups granulated sugar

1/3 cup unsweetened cocoa, sifted

1 1/4 cups evaporated milk

1/2 cup sweet butter or margarine, melted

2 teaspoons pure vanilla extract

Each pie makes 6 generous slices

Snowdrop Pecan Balls

these are quickly made bits of sweetness to serve when you want a taste of something good to enhance your tea cart or to finish a light meal.

Preheat the oven to 300°. Grease 2 cookie sheets.

In a medium bowl, combine the melted margarine or butter and sugar. Add the flour and mix well with a large wooden spoon. Stir in the vanilla extract and nuts; the dough will be stiff.

Form the dough into small balls about the size of a quarter and place about 1 inch apart on prepared pan. Bake for 30 minutes, or until slightly brown around the edges. Cool slightly, then roll the cookies in confectioners' sugar, coating them well. Store in an airtight container.

1 cup margarine or sweet butter, melted

1/3 cup granulated sugar

2 cups self-rising flour

1/2 teaspoon pure vanilla extract

2 cups pecans, finely chopped

Sifted confectioners's sugar for coating

Makes 6 dozen cookies

Christmas Fruitcake Samplers

We call these delicious morsels fruitcake samplers because, in miniature, they have all the rich, mingled flavors of a full-scale holiday fruitcake. There are just enough candied fruits and nuts in the little samplers to give you great fruitcake taste. They're not too sweet, and served with coffee, hot tea, or white wine, they are sheer perfection.

Do not preheat the oven. Grease 2 baking sheets.

Sift together the flour, allspice, and cinnamon and set aside.

In a large bowl, using a wooden spoon, combine the melted margarine and brown sugar. Stir in the beaten eggs and milk. Gradually stir in the dry ingredients and mix well. Add the candied fruits, raisins, dates, and nuts and stir until evenly distributed.

Preheat the oven to 300°.

Drop the batter by teaspoonfuls onto the prepared pans about 1 inch apart. Bake for 25 minutes, or until golden brown. Remove the cookies to a rack to cool.

When the cookies are thoroughly cooled, store in an air-tight container.

1½ cups self-rising flour

½ teaspoon ground allspice

½ teaspoon ground cinnamon

½ cup margarine or sweet butter, melted

½ cup firmly packed light brown sugar

2 large eggs, beaten

¼ cup milk

1 cup red candied cherries, finely chopped

1 cup green candied cherries, finely chopped

1 cup candied pineapple, finely chopped

1 cup raisins

1 cup dates, chopped

3 cups pecans, coarsely chopped

Makes 7 dozen cookies

Benne Seed Wafers

benne seeds, or sesame seeds, were introduced to this country by slaves who were brought to the Carolina coast from West Africa. Benne seeds were planted extensively throughout the South, as plantation owners began growing the seeds for their slaves, who, in turn, used them for food, medicine, and good luck. Eventually benne seed wafers became a Lowcountry specialty—especially at holiday times.

Anyone who eats these wafers is in for a rare treat. Benne Seed Wafers are crisp, spicy, tangy—absolutely wonderful go-alongs with wine or cocktails. Very few Charleston parties are held without them. But you really don't have to have a party to enjoy these wafers. They are always delicious.

1¼ cups all-purpose flour

¼ teaspoon baking powder

¾ cup sweet butter, softened

1½ cups firmly packed light brown sugar

2 large eggs

½ cup benne (sesame) seeds

1 teaspoon pure vanilla extract

Makes 4 dozen cookies

Preheat the oven to 350°. Grease 2 cookie sheets.

Sift the flour and baking powder together. Set aside.

In a medium bowl, cream the butter and brown sugar until fluffy, about 5 minutes. Add the eggs one at a time, beating well after each addition. Stir in the dry ingredients. Stir in the benne seeds and vanilla extract.

Drop the dough by ½ teaspoonfuls onto the greased cookie sheets about 1 inch apart. Bake for 8 to 10 minutes, or until the edges are lightly browned. Remove the cookies to a rack and allow to cool.

Note: If benne seeds are not readily available, use toasted sesame seeds.

Fruit Bran Muffins

muffins are perhaps the quickest way to get toothsome, wholesome goodness to your table—whether at breakfast, tea, or luncheon. These muffins are both delicious and nutritious because of the bran cereal. You can vary the ingredients too, if you like, by adding your family's favorite combinations of fruit and nuts to the batter.

Preheat the oven to 400°. Grease 12 muffin cups or line with paper baking cups.

In a small bowl, mix the bran cereal, brown sugar, and milk. Let stand for 5 minutes.

Sift the flour, baking powder, baking soda, and cinnamon into a large bowl. Stir in the applesauce and egg whites. Stir in the bran mixture. Pour the batter into the prepared muffin cups.

Bake for 20 minutes, or until the muffins are golden brown on top. Remove them from the pans and cool on a rack.

2 cups all-bran cereal

$1/3$ cup firmly packed brown sugar

$1^{1}/_{4}$ cups skim milk

1 cup all-purpose flour

2 teaspoons baking powder

$1/2$ teaspoon baking soda

$1/2$ teaspoon ground cinnamon

$1/2$ cup unsweetened applesauce

2 large egg whites

Makes 12 muffins

Pineapple Muffins

hese delightful muffins were introduced to me at a luau years ago, and I've been serving them as a breakfast treat ever since. The taste is not too sweet and the texture is very light. It's also really hard to eat just one.

Preheat the oven to 350°. Grease 12 muffin cups or line them with paper baking cups.

Sift together the flour, baking powder, and salt and set aside.

In a medium bowl, cream the margarine and sugar until light and fluffy, about 5 minutes. Beat in the eggs one at a time. Beat in the vanilla. Add the flour mixture. Fold in the pineapple.

Pour the batter into the prepared muffin cups, filling them half full. Bake for 20 minutes, or until the muffins are lightly browned on top. Remove the muffins to a cooling rack. Serve warm or at room temperature.

2 cups all-purpose flour

2 teaspoons baking powder

1/2 teaspoon salt

1/2 cup margarine or sweet butter, softened

1 cup granulated sugar

2 large eggs

1 teaspoon pure vanilla extract

1 can (8 ounces) crushed pineapple, undrained, or fresh

Makes 12 muffins

Charleston Tea Bread

many cookbooks include tea breads, but since my recipe actually calls for tea, I like to think it is the REAL thing. The only authentic American tea is grown on Wadmalaw Island, just south of the city, in our very own Carolina Lowcountry, and we are very fortunate to have such an unusual resource right at our doorstep.

The Charleston Tea Company's resident owners, William Hall and Mack Fleming, have revived a unique tradition of tea growing and blending, which began when a French botanist brought the first tea plants to America—to Charleston in 1799.

I like to use this American classic tea in my bread, but you may certainly use your own favorite brew in this recipe. Charleston Tea Bread is a lightly spiced delectable that draws raves every time it is served. It is especially good for breakfast, and makes a delightful housewarming or hostess gift.

$1^{1}/_{4}$ cups firmly packed light brown sugar

1 cup raisins

2 cups cold tea

4 cups self-rising flour

1 teaspoon ground cinnamon

1 teaspoon ground allspice

$^{1}/_{4}$ cup margarine or sweet butter, softened

1 large egg

Makes 8 slices

Combine the brown sugar, raisins, and cold tea in a glass bowl and let sit overnight.

Preheat the oven to 350°. Grease a 9 x 5-inch loaf pan.

Sift the flour and spices together into a large bowl. Add the margarine and egg and mix well. Stir in the soaked raisin mixture.

Pour the batter into the prepared pan. Bake for approximately 1½ hours, or until a cake tester inserted in the middle of the cake comes out clean. Remove the cake from the pan and allow it to cool thoroughly on a rack before slicing.

Huguenot Torte

When we bake and serve this torte here in Charleston, we're not simply offering dessert—we're reliving history!

In the 1700s, thousands of French Huguenots fled to this country to escape persecution. Many came to Charleston, bringing their customs and, of course, their delicious foods.

When St. Andrews Parish Episcopal Church serves this torte during the spring festival of church luncheons, it is a definite favorite.

Preheat the oven to 325°. Grease a 12 x 8-inch pan.

Sift together the flour, baking powder, and salt. Set aside.

In a large mixing bowl, beat the eggs on low speed until thick and lemon-colored, about 4 minutes. Gradually add the sugar. Add the dry ingredients and beat until well mixed. Add the vanilla extract. Gently but thoroughly fold in the nuts and apples.

Pour the batter into the prepared pan. Bake for 45 minutes, or until the torte is crusty and the top is firm and golden brown. (The crust will fall as the torte cools.) Allow the torte to cool in the pan. Cut into squares.

$1/4$ cup all-purpose flour

$2^{1}/_{2}$ teaspoons baking powder

$1/4$ teaspoon salt

2 large eggs

$1^{1}/_{2}$ cups granulated sugar

1 teaspoon pure vanilla extract

1 cup chopped pecans or walnuts

1 cup chopped tart cooking apples

Makes 24 squares

Date-Nut Bars

My best friend, Mary Ann Nelson, often bakes these Date-Nut Bars. Her grandmother taught her to make them when she was a little girl and we are all happy that the recipe has been preserved for generations of Charlestonians. These rich bars melt in your mouth, and the bonus is that the dates are good for you too.

Preheat the oven to 275°. Grease an 8-inch square pan.

Sift the flour and baking powder together. Set aside.

In a medium bowl, mix the butter and brown sugar until creamy. Stir in the eggs, mixing well. Add the flour mixture and the vanilla extract. Fold in the dates and nuts.

Pour the batter into the prepared pan. Bake for 30 minutes, or until the sides come away from the pan.

While the cake is still hot, sprinkle the top generously with sifted confectioners' sugar. Cool the cake in the pan. Cut into squares.

Note: These bars keep well, stored in an airtight container.

1 cup all-purpose flour

1 teaspoon baking powder

1 cup sweet butter (do not substitute margarine), softened

2 cups firmly packed dark brown sugar

2 large eggs

1 teaspoon pure vanilla extract

1 package (8 ounces) pitted dates, coarsely chopped

1 cup pecans, coarsely chopped

Sifted confectioners' sugar for dusting

Makes sixteen 2-inch squares

Fruit Cobbler

We Southerners DO like our fruit desserts! I've never heard a negative word said about a cobbler—especially this one. Its versatility is superseded only by its ease of preparation. And since the ingredients come right from your pantry shelf, it's a marvelous "quickie" when unexpected guests drop in. We like ours served warm, topped with a scoop of vanilla ice cream.

Preheat the oven to 350°.

Melt the margarine in the oven in a 13 x 9-inch pan, making sure that the bottom of the pan is evenly coated. Set aside.

In a medium bowl, mix the sugar, flour, and milk. Spread this mixture evenly over the bottom of the pan. Spoon the pie filling into the pan.

Bake for 35 minutes, or until the cobbler comes away from the sides of the pan. Allow to cool in the pan.

1/2 cup margarine or sweet butter

1 cup granulated sugar

1 cup self-rising flour, sifted

1 cup milk

1 can (20 ounces) pie filling (blueberry, apple, cherry, or peach)

Makes 6 servings

Sadie's Banana Pudding

S adie's banana pudding is the sort of dish that young boys learn to love and continue loving until they are grandfathers. It is made with bananas, vanilla wafers, and real old-fashioned cooked custard. Nobody can eat just one serving. It is Wally's favorite dessert, and since Wally is Sadie's favorite person, we are treated to it fairly often.

In a medium saucepan, beat the egg with a fork or a wire whisk until foamy. Stir in the sugar. Gradually stir in the milk.

Mix the flour with a little water to form a smooth paste (be sure there are no lumps) and add to the egg, sugar, and milk mixture. Cook over very low heat, stirring often, until the custard thickens, 15 to 20 minutes. Add the nutmeg. Remove from the heat.

In a 2-quart baking dish, layer the vanilla wafers and bananas in 2 layers. Pour the custard over the top and let stand for about 1 hour before serving.

1 large egg

$^3/_4$ cup granulated sugar

$2^1/_2$ cups milk

1 tablespoon all-purpose flour

1 teaspoon grated nutmeg

1 box (12 ounces) vanilla wafers

4 small or 3 large bananas

Makes 6 generous servings

classics   67

A Baker's
Dozen
of
Family
Favorites

about our family favorites

billy and I grew up in Charleston, close to the seashore. His family had a summer home on Sullivans Island, about ten miles east of Charleston, in the Atlantic Ocean, and my family owned a summer home approximately twelve miles west of Charleston on Folly Beach. Therefore, as youngsters, we spent every summer in the sun and surf. Those were delightful, fun-filled days, but after Billy and I had been married a while, we decided we had had enough of beach living and were ready for a change.

So, when our son, Wally, was a little boy, we converted half of our yard into a swimming pool. It was a different kind of fun from beach living and ocean swimming, but it was, and still is, fun. The best part is being able to walk out the back door and dive into the pool. No sand, no sticky salty skin, and no crabs underfoot. We can also swim at night, which had always been forbidden by our parents because ocean swimming after dark was considered dangerous.

When Wally was growing up, having a backyard pool meant always having company. And since Wally was a gracious young host, his friends were always welcome. I learned early on to have hot dogs, hamburgers, soft drinks, and sweets in abundance, since young swimmers work up big appetites. Life was busily happy.

But all the fun has not been strictly "child's play." Pool parties have become a way of life for all of us, including adults, during the summer. What a wonderful way to entertain—it's easy, casual, and always a lot of fun. We have enjoyed countless parties with friends and family over the years, but none of them could ever equal our Fourth of July celebration. It was the biggest day in the year for Billy. He really looked forward to having our friends enjoy the day, and being the perfectionist that he was, he was always the perfect host.

Friends and their families would start arriving around noon, bringing babies, lawn chairs, ice chests, towels, and delicious foods of every description. Recipes for many of the desserts we enjoyed then are included in the following pages—Loaf of Bread Cake and Mexican Chocolate Cake were essentials. All of these recipes are easy to make and even easier to eat.

We continue to enjoy our summer fun and the casual pool parties, as well as the delicious goodies. But since Billy's long illness and death, we no longer have our Fourth of July bash. It was HIS day indeed—and we are blessed with such beautiful memories.

Hummingbird Cake

I have never known where the name of this cake came from! Perhaps the originator thought of the brilliant, colorful plumage of the hummingbird as she prepared the bright medley of fruits and nuts for this delicious concoction. At any rate, it's a great favorite of ours.

The tangy zest of Cream Cheese Frosting is a perfect foil for this full-textured and delicately spiced cake. The snowy white topping makes it an ideal choice for a birthday cake, but it really is a fabulous dessert for any occasion.

Do not preheat the oven. Grease and flour a 12-cup tube pan.

Sift together the dry ingredients into a large mixing bowl. Add the eggs and oil and stir until the dry ingredients are evenly moistened. Stir in the vanilla extract, then stir in the bananas, pineapple, and pecans.

Pour the batter into the prepared pan. Set the oven temperature to 350° and bake for 1 hour and 20 minutes, or until a cake tester inserted in the middle of the cake comes out clean. Cool the cake in the pan, then invert onto a serving plate and frost with Cream Cheese Frosting.

3 cups all-purpose flour

2 cups granulated sugar

1 teaspoon baking soda

1 teaspoon ground cinnamon

½ teaspoon salt

3 large eggs, beaten

1 cup vegetable oil

1½ teaspoons pure vanilla extract

2 cups chopped bananas (about 4 medium bananas)

1 can (8 ounces) crushed pineapple, undrained, or fresh

1 cup chopped pecans

Makes 20 slices

Cream Cheese Frosting

Combine the cream cheese, butter and the vanilla extract in a large mixing bowl and beat on low speed until smooth. Gradually add the powdered sugar, and beat on medium speed until light and fluffy, about 10 minutes.

1 package (8 ounces) cream cheese, softened

½ cup sweet butter or margarine, softened

1 teaspoon pure vanilla extract

1 box (1 pound) confectioners' sugar

Makes 4 cups

Pineapple
Upside-Down Cake

Pineapple Upside-Down Cake is easy to make and is always tasty. To make serving easier, I use crushed pineapple instead of the pineapple rings called for in many recipes. The combination of pineapple juice and lemon extract in the batter gives the cake a flavor that is not too sweet and, I think, adds a little zest to this all-time favorite.

Preheat the oven to 350°.

Coat a 13 x 9-inch pan with the melted margarine. Sprinkle the brown sugar over the bottom of the pan.

Drain the pineapple and reserve the juice for the cake batter. Sprinkle the pineapple, chopped nuts, and cherries evenly over the bottom of the pan. Set aside.

pineapple mixture

$1/4$ cup margarine or sweet butter, melted

1 cup firmly packed light brown sugar

1 can (20 ounces) crushed pineapple

1 cup chopped pecans

$1/2$ cup maraschino cherries

In a medium mixing bowl, beat the egg whites until they hold stiff peaks. Set aside.

In a large mixing bowl, beat the margarine or butter and sugar on low speed until light and fluffy, about 5 minutes. Add the egg yolks and mix well. Alternately add the flour and the reserved pineapple juice, mixing well. Fold in the beaten egg whites and then the lemon extract.

Pour the batter over the pineapple mixture in the baking pan. Bake for 25 minutes, or until a tester inserted in the middle of the cake comes out clean. Cool the cake in the pan.

Invert the cooled cake onto a pretty oblong tray and cut into 2-inch squares.

cake

4 large eggs, separated

1 cup margarine or sweet butter, softened

2 cups granulated sugar

3 cups all-purpose flour

1 cup pineapple juice

1 tablespoon lemon extract

Makes 24 squares

Carrot Cake

I never refuse carrot cake. It has a pretty high rating with me, to put it mildly, and over the years I have experimented with hundreds of different recipes. I like this recipe especially for the tangy sweetness of the cinnamon combined with the flavor of the freshly grated carrots that give an unexpected body and richness to the moist texture of the cake. The perfect partner for this unusually luscious Carrot Cake is Orange Glaze.

Preheat the oven to 325°. Grease and flour a 12-cup tube pan.

Sift together the flour, baking powder, cinnamon, and salt.

In a large mixing bowl, combine the oil and sugar and blend on low speed. Add half of the dry ingredients and mix well. Alternately add the eggs and the remaining dry ingredients. Fold in the carrots and nuts just until evenly distributed.

Pour the batter into the prepared pan. Bake for 1 hour and 10 minutes, or until a cake tester inserted in the middle of the cake comes out clean. Cool the cake in the pan.

Invert the cooled cake onto a serving plate and top with Orange Glaze.

2 cups all-purpose flour

2 teaspoons baking powder

2 teaspoons ground cinnamon

1 teaspoon salt

1¼ cups vegetable oil

2 cups granulated sugar

4 large eggs

3 cups grated carrots

1 cup chopped walnuts

Makes 20 large slices

Orange Glaze

Combine all of the ingredients in a small mixing bowl and stir until well blended and smooth. Pour the glaze over the top of the cake and let it drizzle down the sides.

1 cup confectioners' sugar

¼ cup cornstarch

½ teaspoon salt

1 cup orange juice

1 teaspoon fresh lemon juice

Makes about 1½ cups

Carrot Cake—
The Simple Version

Since I'm a real carrot cake person, it had never occurred to me to bake a carrot cake without washing, peeling, and grating carrots. So when Sadie told me about a delicious version of this cake that contains baby food, I looked at her as if she had indeed lost her mind. Sadie is from the old school, and no new idea is ever allowed into her kitchen. I couldn't believe she was actually asking me to put baby food in my mixer. We argued about it for a while and she pouted for an even longer while, and, of course, she won. We baked the cake and, as always, she was right.

This is a mouthwatering cake—moist, not too heavy, and incredibly delicious. For those occasions when a carrot cake is in desperate demand but there is no time to grate fresh carrots, try this simple version. You'll be glad you did, especially if you serve it with Cream Cheese Icing.

cake

2 cups self-rising flour

2 cups granulated sugar

1 teaspoon baking soda

1 teaspoon ground cinnamon

1½ cups vegetable oil

4 large eggs

3 jars (4 ounces each) baby food carrots

Makes 20 large slices

Preheat the oven to 350°. Grease and flour three 8-inch layer cake pans.

Sift the dry ingredients into a large mixing bowl. Add the oil and blend well. Add the eggs one at a time, mixing well after each addition. Stir in the carrots just until blended.

Pour the batter into the prepared pans and bake at 350° for 25 minutes. Cool the layers in the pans for 15 minutes, then invert onto a rack and cool for at least 1 hour.

Frost the cake with Cream Cheese Icing.

Place the cream cheese and margarine in a large mixing bowl. Beating on low speed, gradually add the confectioners' sugar. Increase the speed to medium-high and beat for 4 minutes. Add the vanilla and then the chopped pecans

Spread the icing between the layers and on the top and sides of the thoroughly cooled cake.

cream cheese icing

1 package (8 ounces) cream cheese, softened

1/2 cup margarine, softened

1 box (1 pound) confectioners' sugar

2 teaspoons pure vanilla extract

1 cup chopped pecans

Makes about 4 cups

Mexican Chocolate Cake

recently I had the pleasure of lunching at the Christ Church Tearoom in Mt. Pleasant, South Carolina, just a few short miles from Charleston. The tearoom has helped support the church's many charities since 1976. For two weeks each spring, the parishioners prepare and serve approximately four hundred light lunches a day. Delicious soups, sandwiches, and salads are graciously offered, along with an impressive array of fabulous desserts. Being a real chocolate person, it is never hard for me to make my choice. I always eat every crumb of my serving of Mexican Chocolate Cake, which, thankfully, appears in the tearoom every year.

The key to this chocolate lover's dream is the incredibly rich Hot Fudge Icing that is poured, while it is piping hot, onto the cake when it, too, is still warm. The result is a heavy, moist, fudgey cake—absolutely delicious.

cake

1 cup margarine or sweet butter

¼ cup unsweetened cocoa, sifted

1 cup water

2 cups all-purpose flour

1 teaspoon baking soda

½ teaspoon salt

2 cups granulated sugar

½ cup buttermilk

2 large eggs

1 teaspoon pure vanilla extract

Makes 36 squares

Preheat the oven to 350°. Grease a 12 x 9-inch pan.

In a medium saucepan, melt the margarine. Stir in the cocoa and water and bring to a boil. Set aside.

Sift the flour, baking soda, and salt into a large bowl. Stir in the sugar. Pour the boiled mixture into the bowl and mix well. Add the buttermilk, eggs, and vanilla and mix well.

Pour the batter into the prepared pan and bake for 20 minutes, or until cake tester inserted in the center of the cake comes out clean. While the cake is baking, prepare the icing.

Melt the margarine in a large saucepan. Stir to dissolve the cocoa in the buttermilk and bring to a boil. Remove the saucepan from the heat and gradually add the confectioners' sugar, nuts, and vanilla. Stir well.

Remove the baked cake from the oven and pour the hot icing over the top. Allow the cake to cool in the pan for about 45 minutes. Cut into 2 x 1¼-inch squares and serve.

hot fudge icing

½ cup margarine or sweet butter

¼ cup unsweetened cocoa

¼ cup plus 2 tablespoons buttermilk

1 box (1 pound) confectioners' sugar

½ cup chopped pecans or walnuts

1 teaspoon pure vanilla extract

Makes 4 cups

Loaf of Bread Cake

Old-Fashioned Chocolate Layer Cake

O f all the desserts that I dearly love—and that covers a wide range—my lifelong favorite is still old-fashioned chocolate layer cake— white layer cake with chocolate frosting. At least I always thought it was called chocolate layer cake until I was reeducated a few years ago by our little next-door neighbor. As his birthday approached, I asked him what kind of birthday cake he would like. His answer was "Loaf of Bread Cake." No amount of questioning could help me understand what he meant until I asked his mother. Her response was "Oh, Timmy's favorite cake is chocolate layer cake. You know, white cake with chocolate icing. Timmy thinks it looks like a loaf of bread with chocolate icing." His name stuck, and we hope you will enjoy our Loaf of Bread Cake.

cake

3 cups all-purpose flour

1¼ teaspoons baking powder

¾ teaspoon salt

1 cup sweet butter, softened

2 cups granulated sugar

½ teaspoon pure almond extract

4 large eggs

1 cup milk

Makes 16 unbelievably good slices

Preheat the oven to 350°. Grease and flour three 8-inch layer cake pans.

Sift together the flour, baking powder, and salt. Set aside.

In a large mixing bowl, beat the butter on low speed until creamy, about 2 minutes. Gradually add the sugar and beat until light and fluffy, about 5 minutes. Add the almond extract. Add the eggs one at a time, beating well after each addition. Alternately add the sifted dry ingredients and milk, blending well.

Pour the batter into the prepared pans and bake for 20 minutes, or until layers are golden brown on top. Invert the layers onto a cake rack to cool completely.

Frost the cooled cake with Chocolate Frosting.

Sift the sugar and cocoa together.

In a large mixing bowl, blend the butter and the sugar mixture on low speed. Gradually add the milk. Increase the speed to medium and beat until the frosting is smooth and creamy, about 5 minutes. Increase the mixer speed to medium-high and beat for about 10 minutes or until spreadable, scraping the bowl often. Reduce the speed to low and add the vanilla.

chocolate frosting

1 box (4 cups) confectioners' sugar

1½ cups unsweetened cocoa

1 cup sweet butter

1 cup evaporated milk

1 teaspoon pure vanilla extract

Makes 6 cups

Fruitcake

Originally, our family fruitcake recipe came from my father. We never knew whether it was his mother's recipe, or whether he simply made it up. But, bless his heart, fruitcake baking in our family was his territory and nobody invaded. Once a year, around December 1, he made a career of baking his fruitcakes. He began early—buying, chopping, storing—preparing the myriad fruits for the big day. The whole process was costly, exhausting, and just plain awful! By the time he had added figs, currants, and dates (and every other dark fruit he could find) to the mix, the finished cake would come out black and tasting bitter.

I truly don't think he liked it any better than we did, and with a little gentle persuasion, he was finally convinced to abandon his recipe and try a different one. This is the recipe that evolved. We think it is delicious. In addition to candied fruit and nuts, it contains orange juice and maraschino cherries to help make the cake moist. And I think the "extra" pound of golden raisins contributes to its overall goodness. Heavy, moist, and loaded with fruits and nuts, it is our family favorite. Serve it with a glass of wine—can you think of a nicer holiday treat?

Do not preheat the oven. Grease two 10-cup tube pans and line the bottoms with brown paper.

Sift the flour into a large bowl. Stir in the nuts, raisins, and candied fruit. Set aside.

In a large mixing bowl, beat the butter and sugar on low speed for about 8 minutes until light and fluffy. Add the eggs one at a time, mixing well after each addition. Using a large wooden spoon, stir in the maraschino cherries, with their juice, and the orange juice.

Gradually add the flour mixture, mixing well. (The batter will be stiff.)

Spoon the batter into the prepared pans, filling each one about three-quarters full. Set the oven temperature to 250° and bake for 1½ to 2 hours, or until the tops of the cakes are brown and the sides come away from the pans. Cool the cakes in the pans. Make sure the cakes have cooled completely before removing them from the pans; they are fragile while still hot.

4¼ cups all-purpose flour

1 pound almonds, chopped

1 pound pecans, chopped

2 pounds golden raisins

1½ pounds candied pineapple, diced

1 pound candied cherries, diced

1 pound sweet butter (do not substitute margarine), softened

2¼ cups granulated sugar

10 large eggs

1 jar (8 ounces) maraschino cherries, chopped

½ cup fresh orange juice

Makes 2 large cakes; 20 slices each

Sadie's Bread Pudding

n o book from our bakery would be complete without one of Sadie's specialties. Sadie seldom shares her recipes because, as she says, "I don't measure anything, you know." But she was flattered to be included in the book and immediately began talking about how to put her bread pudding in writing. It wasn't easy. She really does NOT measure. But this approximation is as accurate as possible.

Sadie's Bread Pudding is light, creamy, and puffy around the edges. It almost melts in your mouth and needs no serving help except a pretty compote and a spoon.

Preheat the oven to 350°.

Tear the bread into bite-sized pieces and set aside.

In a medium bowl, beat the egg until foamy. Add the sugar and stir until well blended. Add the bread and stir until it is well moistened. Gradually add the milk. Add the nutmeg, cinnamon, vanilla extract, and margarine and stir.

Pour the mixture into a 2-quart baking dish. Bake for 45 minutes, or until the top is golden brown.

4 slices white bread

1 large egg

³/₄ cup granulated sugar

2 cups skim milk

¹/₄ teaspoon grated nutmeg

¹/₄ teaspoon ground cinnamon

¹/₂ teaspoon pure vanilla extract

1 tablespoon low-fat margarine, melted

Makes 6 servings

Pumpkin Bread

Pumpkin bread is one of those in-between treats. It isn't exactly bread, but it isn't exactly cake either. We like to serve it for breakfast with cream cheese. Baked in small pans, these mini loaves are popular on breakfast buffets and make excellent gifts. I keep some in my freezer at all times—for gifts, basket stuffers, or for just plain eating.

Preheat the oven to 350°. Grease 5 mini (5 x 3-inch) loaf pans.

Sift together the flour and cinnamon. Set aside.

In a medium bowl, stir the sugar and oil until just blended. Add the eggs, egg whites, and pumpkin and stir until thoroughly mixed. Add the dry ingredients and raisins and mix well.

Pour the batter into the prepared pans. Bake for 25 to 30 minutes or until the loaves begin to come away from the sides of the pans. Allow the loaves to cool in the pans for about 15 minutes, then invert onto racks to cool. Do not slice until completely cooled.

2 cups self-rising flour

1 tablespoon ground cinnamon

1½ cups granululed sugar

¾ cup canola or vegetable oil

2 large eggs

2 large egg whites

1 can (16 ounces) solid pack pumpkin (not pie mix)

1 cup raisins

Makes 5 mini loaves

Blueberry Corn Muffins

Who would have thought of combining corn muffins and blueberries? Not I. But I'm grateful for the idea. It is a delightful combination. Blueberry Corn Muffins can be served as a breakfast treat, or, because they are only mildly sweet, as a dinner bread. I can eat them anytime.

Preheat the oven to 400°. Grease 12 large muffin cups or line with paper liners.

Reserve 1 tablespoon of the brown sugar. Sift the flour, the remaining sugar, the cornmeal, baking powder, baking soda, and salt together. Set aside.

In a large mixing bowl, stir together the yogurt, egg substitute, water, melted margarine, and vanilla extract. Add the dry ingredients and mix only until well moistened. Gently fold in the blueberries.

Spoon the batter into the prepared muffin cups, filling them about two-thirds full. Sprinkle with the reserved sugar. Bake for 15 minutes, or until lightly browned. Cool the muffins on a rack.

⅔ cup firmly packed light brown sugar

4 cups all-purpose flour

½ cup yellow cornmeal

2 teaspoons baking powder

2 teaspoons baking soda

½ teaspoon salt

2 cups vanilla nonfat yogurt

½ cup egg substitute

¼ cup water

¼ cup margarine or sweet butter, melted

2 teaspoons pure vanilla extract

2 cups blueberries

Makes 12 muffins

Buttermilk Coffee Cake

If there is a universal favorite in our household, it's homemade breakfast bread. Of the many different kinds of bread we enjoy, our favorite is Buttermilk Coffee Cake. The trouble is, its texture is so light, one serving is never enough! And since this recipe doesn't yield a big cake, I usually serve it when the crowd is thin.

Preheat the oven to 375°. Grease an 8-inch square pan.

Sift together the flour, sugar, baking powder, ½ teaspoon of the cinnamon, and the salt into a large mixing bowl. Cut in the margarine with 2 knives until the mixture resembles coarse crumbs.

Reserve ½ cup of this crumb mixture. Add the remaining ½ teaspoon cinnamon to the remaining crumb mixture. Dissolve the baking soda in the buttermilk and add to the crumb mixture, stirring until the dry ingredients are well moistened. Add the vanilla extract.

Pour the batter into the prepared pan. Sprinkle with the reserved crumb mixture. Bake for 35 minutes, or until the cake is lightly browned on top.

Cool the cake in the pan. Cut it into squares when the cake is completely cool.

2 cups all-purpose flour

1 cup granulated sugar

½ teaspoon baking powder

1 teaspoon ground cinnamon

¼ teaspoon salt

½ cup margarine or sweet butter, softened

½ teaspoon baking soda

¾ cup buttermilk

1 teaspoon pure vanilla extract

**Makes twelve
2⅔ x 2-inch squares**

Glazed Cranberry
Coffee Cake

O ne of my best friends used to say that she loved cranberry sauce so much she could even eat it on corn bread. In an effort to avoid such a grim happening, I set out to develop something for her that was not corn bread, and the result was Cranberry Coffee Cake. We think it makes an excellent breakfast treat because it is not too sweet. Sour cream and cranberry sauce help keep it moist. And my friend loves it! Top it with a simple glaze.

cake

2 cups all-purpose flour

1 teaspoon baking powder

1 teaspoon baking soda

1/2 teaspoon salt

1/2 cup margarine or sweet butter, softened

1 cup granulated sugar

1 teaspoon pure vanilla extract

2 large eggs

1 cup sour cream

1 cup whole-berry cranberry sauce

1/3 cup chopped walnuts or pecans

Makes 18 slices

Preheat the oven to 350°. Grease and flour a 12-cup tube pan.

Sift together the dry ingredients. Set aside.

In a large mixing bowl, beat the margarine, the sugar, and vanilla extract on low speed until light and fluffy, about 5 minutes. Add the eggs, beating well after each addition. Alternately add the dry ingredients and sour cream, mixing well.

Pour half the batter into the prepared pan. Spoon half of the cranberry sauce over the batter. Pour the remaining batter over sauce. Top with the remaining cranberry sauce. Swirl a knife through the batter to marble it. Sprinkle the nuts on top. Bake for 50 minutes, or until a cake tester inserted in the middle of the cake comes out clean.

While the cake is cooling, mix the glaze.

In a small bowl mix the sugar and vanilla extract. Stir in just enough warm water to make a soft mixture. Drizzle the glaze over the top of the cooled cake, letting it run down the sides.

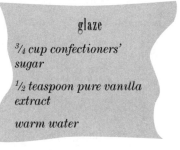

glaze

¾ cup confectioners' sugar

½ teaspoon pure vanilla extract

warm water

Makes about ¾ cup

Special Apple Coffee Cake

In this recipe, cinnamon-coated apples mix beautifully with a mildly orange-flavored batter to create a delicious breakfast treat. Served warm or cold, it's a fabulous snack for ANY time of the day.

Do not preheat the oven. Grease and flour a 12-cup tube pan.

Combine 2 cups of the sugar, the cinnamon, and apples in a medium bowl. Set aside.

Sift the flour and baking powder into a large mixing bowl. Add the remaining ¼ cup plus 1 tablespoon sugar, the oil, and orange juice. Mix on low speed for 1 minute. Add the eggs one at a time, mixing well after each addition. Add the vanilla extract.

Pour half of the batter into the pan. Spoon half of the apple mixture on top of the batter. Pour the remaining batter over the apples. Spoon the remaining apple mixture over the top. Set the oven temperature to 350° and bake for 1 hour, or until a cake tester inserted in the middle of the cake comes out clean. Cool the cake in the pan.

2¼ cups plus 1 tablespoon granulated sugar

2 teaspoons ground cinnamon

6 medium apples, peeled and cut into bite-size pieces

3 cups all-purpose flour

2½ teaspoons baking powder

1 cup vegetable oil

¼ cup fresh orange juice

4 large eggs

1 teaspoon pure vanilla extract

Makes 20 slices

Snacks
and
Picnic
Treats

about our snacks
and picnic treats

One of my greatest pleasures was my association with the Political Science Department at the College of Charleston. How many of us look forward to going to work each day? I did, every day, and I think that says it all: not to dread the coming workday but, rather, to anticipate yet another pleasant one among friends and co-workers.

When I was transferred from the Alumni Affairs Office to that esteemed department, with its varied group of academicians, I was welcomed with open arms by the entire staff. Although I had served as an instructor of secretarial sciences at the technical college, I had never worked in a strictly academic environment and did not know what to expect. Perhaps I thought that these highly educated professors would have neither the time nor the inclination for informality or camaraderie. But I was pleasantly surprised. From their easy banter with each other, and their interaction with the students, I learned very quickly that there would be good times ahead. We worked hard, but it was pleasant work and my days there were happy. These wonderful people soon became my "other family."

There was always a fresh pot of coffee brewing and, of course, some kind of accompanying snack. Sometimes a professor's wife would send in some baked goodies; sometimes we would have apples brought by a weekend mountain traveler. One lady even brought a big basket of fresh tomatoes and cucumbers from her husband's garden. So we always had something to share, and share we did. Our office door was always open to faculty, staff, and students.

Birthdays were big days for us. We celebrated everybody's birthday with something from the Charleston Cake Lady. It was during this time that my mail-order business really began to flourish, and this other family of mine was happy for me. They were even more excited than I was when I received an order for two gift cakes to be sent to Mrs. Robert F. Kennedy. What a wonderful group of friends and co-workers. My memories of them are precious.

In the pages that follow, I have included recipes for many of the fun foods we shared and enjoyed during one of the happiest interludes of my life. It is my hope that these recipes will bring you some of the joy I felt in sharing them with my other family.

These recipes are fun to bake and easy to transport. Popular with young and old alike, they are wonderful for at-home (especially outdoor) parties, and they will put the finishing touch on your picnic basket.

Tip: Be sure to store these treats in airtight containers, or wrap them in several layers of plastic wrap before putting them in plastic food bags. They dry out very quickly when exposed to the air, and I want you to have fresh goodies when you say, "Have Fun Food, Will Travel."

About Chews

When asked by my charming and perfectly delightful editor, "What exactly is a chew?" my immediate reaction was "Oh dear, are there people who have never enjoyed chews?" But after a bit of rationalizing, I have decided that everyone has eaten chews—in one form or another—or has known them, perhaps, by another name. I hope so.

Not unlike brownies, our chews are bar cookies, baked in a rectangular pan, then cut into squares. The batter usually contains brown sugar but not chocolate. The texture is dense, moist, and chewy (hence, the name), and nuts provide richness and crunch.

By whatever name they are known to you, I'm sure you have enjoyed chews —everybody does.

Charleston Chews

ever since I can remember, we have baked and enjoyed what we call Chinese Chews, without ever really knowing how the Chinese got all the credit for these delicious morsels. When we started baking our own version of these chews years ago, Wally's comment was "Well, we Charlestonians eat rice and worship our ancestors, just like the Chinese people do. Now we've stolen their chews." Perhaps. (But I think not.)

My recipe for Charleston Chews came from our next-door neighbor, and I have never known anyone who didn't like them. I would guess that we have received more requests for this recipe than any other—ever! They really are delicious. And even with no shortening, they are moist and chewy.

Preheat the oven to 350°. Grease a 13 x 9-inch pan.

In a large bowl, mix the eggs, brown sugar, flour, and vanilla extract until well blended. Fold in the nuts.

Pour the batter into the prepared pan. Bake for 25 minutes, or until golden brown on top. Sprinkle the chews with sifted confectioners' sugar. Cut into squares when cool, and wait for the raves.

4 large eggs

1 box (1 pound) dark brown sugar

2½ cups self-rising flour, sifted

1 teaspoon pure vanilla extract

1 cup chopped walnuts or pecans

Sifted confectioners' sugar for dusting

Makes thirty-six 2 x 1 1/2-inch squares

Chocolate Chip Chews

m uch of my life has been spent on the campus of the College of Charleston. It is one of the country's most beautiful schools, and I treasure the hours of pleasure it has afforded me. I was a student at the College of Charleston in the 1940s, when the school was quite small. The student body averaged approximately four hundred students and everybody knew everybody. As a freshman, I pledged Phi Mu Fraternity—college life had begun.

In those days, we did not have a sorority house like the large antebellum house used today by the College of Charleston Phi Mus. We had a series of small rooms, grungy little holes-in-the-wall that were constantly in need of refurbishing. But we thought they were fine and spent as much time there as possible. We even answered our phone, "This is Heaven, to which little Phi Mu angel do you wish to speak?" There were lots of parties—girls' parties, coed parties, house parties on the beach—and we always had chocolate chip chews. They are dense, moist, and chewy. The combination of brown sugar, chocolate chips, and nuts just can't be beat. In my little world, they have become a classic.

Preheat the oven to 350°. Grease a 13 x 9-inch pan.

In a medium bowl, stir the melted margarine or butter and brown sugar just until the sugar is evenly moistened. Add the beaten eggs and mix well. Stir in the sifted flour. Fold in the nuts and chocolate morsels. Add the vanilla extract.

Pour the batter into the prepared pan and bake for 30 minutes, or until the top is lightly browned. Cool in the pan, then cut into squares.

Note: Our Chocolate Chip Chews are quickly and easily made on short notice. Because they are so portable, they are great for picnics. They won't crumble in your picnic basket, and you won't have any left to carry home.

½ cup margarine or sweet butter, melted

2 cups firmly packed light brown sugar

2 large eggs, well beaten

2 cups self-rising flour, sifted

1 cup chopped walnuts or pecans

8 ounces semisweet chocolate chips

1 teaspoon pure vanilla extract

Makes approximately forty-eight 1½-inch squares

Chocolate Date Squares

as I write about these delightfully scrumptious treats, I am saddened that their originator is no longer with us. They were developed by my dearest friend, Ann Gilmore, who not only baked them with ease, but shared them with pleasure. Very often, with no warning and for no special reason, Ann would appear with a tin of Chocolate Date Squares.

Because Ann so generously kept us supplied with them, I scarcely ever had to bake them myself. But they are very easy to make. The dates and chocolate combine beautifully for a distinctive taste. They make a handsome addition to a party tray and a very special bedtime snack with a glass of milk. In sum, they are good anytime—anywhere.

Ann's fun-loving personality was highlighted by her generosity. She would have been so happy to share her specialty with you.

1 cup all-purpose flour

1 teaspoon baking powder

1/2 teaspoon salt

1 cup granulated sugar

2 large eggs

2 teaspoons sweet butter or margarine, melted

1 tablespoon plus 1 teaspoon hot water

1 package (8 ounces) dates, chopped

1 cup semisweet chocolate chips

3/4 cup chopped pecans

Makes forty-eight 1 1/2-inch squares

Preheat the oven to 325°.

Grease a 13 x 9-inch pan.

Sift together the flour, baking powder, and salt. Set aside.

In a medium bowl, mix the sugar and eggs until light and fluffy. Add the melted butter, water, dates, chocolate chips, and the flour mixture. Mix well.

Pour the batter into the prepared pan. Sprinkle the nuts over the top. Bake for 30 minutes, or until the top is golden brown. Cool in the pan, then cut into squares.

Walnut Kisses

the Walnut Kiss is somewhere between a candy and a cookie. These little morsels simply melt in your mouth, and they always draw raves. Be prepared to offer seconds—and thirds—because to eat one is to want several more. They are perfect for parties, and make wonderful munchies. For a refreshing treat or a bedtime snack, serve them with a glass of cold milk

Preheat the oven to 300°. Line a cookie sheet with aluminum foil.

In a medium bowl, beat the eggs whites until they are stiff but not dry. Gradually beat in the sugar. Fold in the vanilla. Fold in the walnuts and salt.

Drop the mixture by heaping teaspoonfuls onto the prepared pan about 1 inch apart. Bake for 30 minutes: To test for doneness, lift one kiss from the pan with a spatula and let it stand for 1 minute. If it holds its shape, remove the cookies from the oven; if not, bake for several minutes longer. Cool the cookies on a cake rack.

3 large egg whites

1 cup granulated sugar

1 teaspoon pure vanilla extract

1 cup finely chopped walnuts

¼ teaspoon salt

Makes 24 cookies

Cranberry Squares

Since my family loves the taste of cranberries, I decided to try my hand at inventing a dessert that would capture their sweet and tangy flavor. The result was Cranberry Squares. They are light in texture and not too sweet. And even though they contain no shortening, they are delightfully moist. The lemon juice provides the zest, and the nuts provide the crunch to make a delicious breakfast treat or a great snack any time of the day. These little delectables freeze well, and they make excellent gifts. I try to keep some in my freezer at all times, ready to be popped into a basket or a pretty tin on a moment's notice.

Preheat the oven to 350°. Grease a 13 x 9-inch pan.

Sift the flour into a large mixing bowl. Stir in the sugar.

In a medium bowl, beat the egg and egg whites until foamy. Add the lemon juice. Stir this mixture into the dry ingredients until well blended. Stir in the cranberry sauce. Fold in the nuts.

Pour the batter into the prepared pan and bake for 30 minutes, or until the top is lightly browned. Cool the cake in the pan. Cut into squares when completely cool.

3 cups self-rising flour

1⅓ cups granulated sugar

1 large egg

3 large egg whites

2 tablespoons fresh lemon juice

1 can (16 ounces) jellied cranberry sauce

1½ cups coarsely chopped walnuts

Makes forty-eight 1½-inch squares

Old-Fashioned Brownies

I have been using this brownie recipe for about fifty years, and we still love it. The deep chocolate richness and light cakey texture are especially appealing. They are not quite as chewy as some other versions, but they are sinfully delicious. My only complaint is that they don't yield enough for a truly chocolate-hungry group. Serve these when the crowd is thin, or make two batches.

Preheat the oven to 350°. Grease an 8-inch square pan.

Melt the chocolate in a double-boiler; let cool.

In a medium bowl, beat the eggs until foamy. Stir in the sugar, chocolate, oil, and vanilla extract. Mix until well blended. Gradually add the sifted flour. Fold in the nuts.

Pour the batter into the prepared pan and bake for 30 minutes, or until the sides come away from the pan. Allow the brownies to cool in the pan before cutting into 1½-inch squares.

2 squares (1 ounce each) unsweetened baking chocolate (do not use sweet or semisweet chocolate)

2 large eggs

1 cup granulated sugar

⅔ cup vegetable oil

1 teaspoon pure vanilla extract

1 cup self-rising flour, sifted

1 cup chopped pecans

Makes 12

Peanut Butter Brownies

any combination of peanut butter and chocolate will always suit me. Of course, some combinations are better than others—and these peanut butter brownies fall into the very best category. I try not to bake them too often since my willpower is so poor.

Preheat the oven to 350°. Grease a 9 x 13-inch pan.

Sift together the flour and salt. Set aside.

Sift the cocoa and baking soda into a large mixing bowl. Add ⅓ cup of the melted butter and blend well. Stir in the boiling water until the mixture is smooth. Beat in the sugar, eggs, and the remaining ⅓ cup melted butter, mixing until smooth. Add the dry ingredients and vanilla extract and mix well. Gently fold in the peanut butter chips.

Pour the batter into the prepared pan. Bake for 30 minutes, or until the top is golden brown. Allow the brownies to cool completely in the pan before cutting into squares.

1½ cups all-purpose flour

¼ teaspoon salt

¾ cup unsweetened cocoa

½ teaspoon baking soda

⅔ cup sweet butter, melted

½ cup boiling water

2 cups granulated sugar

2 large eggs

1 teaspoon pure vanilla extract

2 cups peanut butter chips

Makes forty-eight 1½-inch squares

Fruitcake Bars

I t wouldn't be Christmas at our house without making a traditional fruit-cake. We usually take pride and pleasure in performing the ritual of bak-ing one, lacing it with brandy, and storing it to mellow. But sometimes, because of today's fast pace, we slip up between Thanksgiving and Christmas and don't get this pleasant chore done. When that happens—or when we want a taste of Christmas in July or October—we whip up these quick and easy, but equally won-derful, Fruitcake Bars.

This recipe was developed especially for the weekends we spent with close friends—six couples who, for more than half a century, regularly escaped Charleston's Indian summer with a retreat to the cool mountains of North Carolina.

One would have thought there were no food vendors in North Carolina, judging by the amount of food we carried from Charleston. We impressed even ourselves with our culinary feats—to the extent that we prepared our own little in-house recipe booklet, RECIPES FROM SAPPHIRE VALLEY.

Heavy with fruit and nuts, these bars are rich and dense. The vanilla-almond combination complements the brown sugar to create a truly delicious confection.

Do not preheat the oven. Grease and flour a 13 x 9-inch pan.

In a medium bowl, beat the butter and brown sugar until creamy, about 5 minutes. Add the eggs one at a time, mixing well after each addition. Blend in the flour and vanilla and almond extracts, mixing well. Fold in the nuts.

Pour the batter into the prepared pan. Piece by piece, press the fruit into the batter, placing the pieces as close together as possible. Set the oven temperature to 250° and bake for 1½ hours, or until a cake tester inserted in the middle of the cake comes out clean. Cool the cake in the pan. Cut into bars.

½ cup sweet butter (do not substitute margarine)

1½ cups firmly packed dark brown sugar

2 large eggs

1 cup self-rising flour, sifted

1 tablespoon pure vanilla extract

1 teaspoon pure almond extract

2 cups chopped pecans

8 ounces candied cherries, cut into bite-size pieces

8 ounces candied pineapple, cut into bite-size pieces

1 box (18 ounces) dates, cut into bite-size pieces

Makes thirty-six 2 x 1½-inch bars

Teresa's Brownies

Since I love brownies better than any other food I know, we have many versions of them in our files. This one, a composite of several recipes, is my favorite. We combined oil and margarine for added moistness and used more eggs than most recipes, making the mixture extremely rich. The finished product is a dense, rich, moist brownie that has caused us to fight over the last one.

Preheat the oven to 350°. Grease a 13 x 9-inch pan.

Sift together the flour, cocoa, baking soda, and salt. Set aside.

In a large bowl, combine the oil and melted margarine. Stir in the dry ingredients and sugar until well blended. Add the eggs and the vanilla and almond extracts and stir gently until smooth. Fold in the nuts.

Pour the batter into the prepared pan. Bake for 25 minutes, or until the sides have come away from the pan. Allow the brownies to cool in the pan. Cut into squares when cool.

2 cups all-purpose flour

$^3/_4$ cup unsweetened cocoa

$^1/_2$ teaspoon baking soda

$^1/_4$ teaspoon salt

$^1/_4$ cup vegetable oil

1 cup margarine or sweet butter, melted

2 cups granulated sugar

4 large eggs

1 teaspoon pure vanilla extract

$^1/_4$ teaspoon pure almond extract

1 cup chopped pecans or walnuts

Makes forty-eight $1^1/_2$-inch squares

Index

Burros, Marian, xii, 23
buttermilk:
    in Carolina orange date-nut
        cake, 51
    coffee cake, 89
    in hot fudge icing, 81
    in Mexican chocolate cake,
        80–81

C
cake mixes, prepared, 17
cakes:
    applesauce, 38
    banana pineapple, 39
    best devil's food, 44
    blackberry wine, 37
    black walnut, 32–33
    brown sugar nut, 30–31
    carrot, 76
    carrot—the simple version,
        78–79
    chocolate chip, 23
    chocolate chip cheesecake, 43
    coconut carrot, 36
    fruited spice, 34–35
    gem, 20–21
    heavenly coconut, 48
    hummingbird, 72
    loaf of bread (old-fashioned
        chocolate layer), 82–83
    macaroon, 22
    Mexican chocolate, 80–81
    milk chocolate, 26–27
    old-fashioned chocolate layer
        (loaf of bread), 82–83

pineapple upside-down, 74–75
poppyseed, 24–25
punch bowl, 50
sherry nut, 29
spice, 40
vanilla wafer, 28
see also coffee cakes; fruit-
    cake; nut cakes; pound
    cakes; spice cake
candied cherries:
    in Christmas fruitcake sam-
        plers, 57
    in fruitcake, 84–85
    in fruitcake bars, 106–107
candied pineapple:
    in Christmas fruitcake sam-
        plers, 57
    in fruitcake, 84–85
    in fruitcake bars, 106–107
Carolina orange date-nut cake,
    51
carrot cake, 76
    coconut, 36
    the simple version, 78–79
Charleston chews, 97
Charleston classics, 41–68
    benne seed wafers, 58–59
    best devil's food cake, 44–45
    Carolina orange date-nut cake,
        51
    Charleston tea bread, 62–63
    chocolate chess pies, 55
    chocolate chip cheesecake,
        43

Christmas fruitcake samplers,
    57
coconut pie, 54
cranberry banana pie, 52
date-nut bars, 65
fruit bran muffins, 60
fruit cobbler, 66
gardenia pie, 53
heavenly coconut cake, 48–49
Huguenot torte, 64
Lowcountry nut cake, 46
Old South nut cake, 47
punch bowl cake, 50
pineapple muffins, 61
Sadie's banana pudding,
    67
snowdrop pecan rolls, 56
Charleston tea bread, 62–63
Charleston Tea Company, 62
Charlestowne pound cake, 8–9
cheesecake, chocolate chip, 43
cherries, candied:
    in Christmas fruitcake sam-
        plers, 57
    in fruitcake, 84–85
    in fruitcake bars, 106–107
cherries, maraschino:
    in fruitcake, 84–85
    in pineapple upside-down
        cake, 74–75
cherry pie filling:
    in fruit cobbler, 66
    in punch bowl cake, 50
chess pies, chocolate, 55

To contact the Cake Lady:

Teresa Pregnall
774 Woodward Road
Charleston, South Carolina 29407
(803) 763-2551